Embroidered
Treasures * FOR CHILDREN *

Embroidered
Treasures * FOR CHILDREN *

CLAIRE GARLAND

STC CRAFT | A MELANIE FALICK BOOK

NEW YORK

For Harry, May, and James—thanks for your inspiration.

Copyright © 2005 Octopus Publishing Group Limited

Text, illustrations, and photographs copyright © 2005 Claire and John Garland

Published in 2005 by
Stewart, Tabori & Chang
115 West 18th Street
New York, NY 10011
www.abramsbooks.com

Canadian Distribution:
Canadian Manda Group
165 Dufferin Street
Toronto, Ontario M6K 3H6
Canada

Library of Congress Cataloging-in-Publication Data
Garland, Claire.
    Embroidered treasures for children / by Claire Garland.
        p. cm.
Includes index.
    ISBN 1-58479-430-5
1. Embroidery—Patterns. 2. Infants' supplies. 3. Children's paraphernalia. I. Title.
    TT775.G37 2005
    746.44'041—dc22
                                                2005008739

Photography, illustration, and design by John Garland

The text of this book was composed in Gill Sans and Voluta Script

Color origination by Chroma Graphics (Overseas) Pte Ltd., Singapore
Printed and bound in China by Toppan Printing Company Ltd.

10 9 8 7 6 5 4 3 2 1

First Printing

Stewart, Tabori & Chang is a subsidiary of

LA MARTINIÈRE
G R O U P E

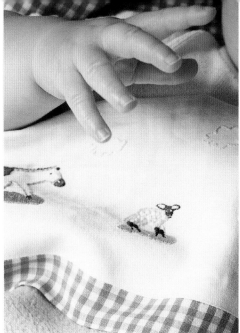

CONTENTS

introduction 7

Introduction

EMBROIDERING FOR CHILDREN is not only the most perfectly satisfying way to spend your day, it also gives undeniable pleasure to the young recipient. There is no doubt that such a gift, personally made and however small, will be one that is cherished forever. Indeed, every one of the treasures in this book has been carefully chosen with children very much in mind, and tried and tested by my own.

The book contains a plethora of projects, from toys to bedding, and from slippers to beach bags. You will find cuddly animals, adventurous sailors, dreamy fairies, and vintage flowers among the designs. My aim has been to design special things to add to, not replace, children's favorites – certainly not to pretend to be any other toy sold in stores today. The book also represents a return to the traditional values of taking time out to have a hobby and create something, which in turn satisfies the soul. In fact, it would be marvelous if this book inspired you to create using your own ideas.

Each project can be completed within a few weeks of starting – some in a matter of days! The projects are organized so that even if you have never embroidered in your life, starting this new hobby will not be a daunting prospect. If you are an experienced embroiderer, the book will simply provide you with a fresh approach and plenty of inspiration. As with all homemade items, let common sense be your guide. Take care to remove all pins when the project is completed and sew all buttons and embellishments securely. Never leave a baby unsupervised with a blanket or any child alone with a project that includes an embellishment.

The art of giving gifts or presenting your hard work is almost as important as the process of making – a beautifully wrapped, homemade, scrumptious-looking parcel is a token of your affection. The best and most effective way of wrapping any gift is with style and simplicity – less is more. Layer each item with tissue paper and choose plain, good-quality papers and ribbons or ties to hide the treasure waiting within. Complete your gift with a special handmade tag to express your greeting and love.

Claire Garland

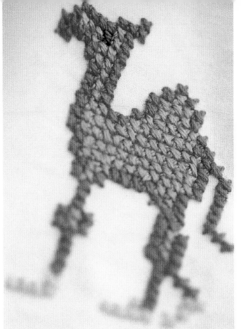
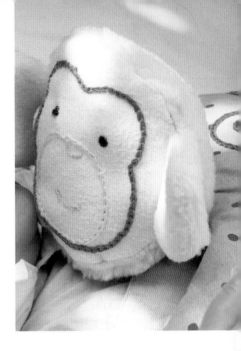

CHAPTER ONE comfort and calm

This selection of gentle and soothing items is dedicated to babies everywhere. Protecting them in a variety of comforting designs and calming colors may be as near as you can get to cradling them in comfort.

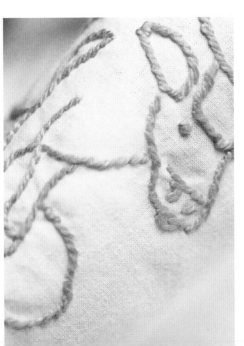

how to make

NOAH crib sheet and blanket

Cuddly animals frisk along a crisp white sheet — clean and cool to wrap your sleepy newborn baby in.

The delicate palette and soft texture of cotton on cotton give this design a sense of cool comfort.

FINISHED SIZE **Crib sheet:** approximately 40"x60" (100cm x150cm)

Crib blanket: crib-sized knitted baby blanket

MATERIALS AND TOOLS

• DMC stranded embroidery cotton in the following shades:

one skein of each color: **162** ice; **210** lilac; **310** black; **433** brown; **702** grass; **742** orange; **778** light mauve; **954** pistachio; **976** caramel; **996** turquoise; **3328** dark peach; **3821** sunflower; **3823** vanilla

For the sheet

• Plain white cotton crib sheet

• 4¾"x32" (12cm x80cm) of 14-count waste canvas

• Water-soluble marker

• Ruler

• Crewel needle, size 9

• Embroidery hoop

• Contrasting thread for basting and marker stitches

For the blanket

• Plain stockinette stitch blanket, hand-knit or bought

• Tapestry needle, size 24

TECHNIQUES For cross stitch, see page 118. For using waste canvas and reading the chart, see page 115.

STITCHES USED Counted cross stitch

How to begin your sheet

1 Fold the top edge of the sheet in half lengthwise to find the center. Press and mark it with a basting stitch or two.

2 Determine the baseline along which the motifs will be spaced by turning the top edge of the sheet over by 6" (15cm), along the grain of the fabric. Press the fold. Mark the baseline with a row of basting stitches or a ruled line made with the water-soluble marker.

3 Find the center of the strip of waste canvas by folding it in half widthwise. Place the fold over the center fold on the sheet and align the canvas with the baseline, allowing ¾" (2cm) of the canvas to fall below the line.

4 Pin and baste the canvas, working a few diagonal stitches to hold it in place.

Working the embroidery

1 The entire design is worked with two strands of thread. Begin the cross stitch following the chart on pages 14–15: The red lines indicate where to join the overlapping sections of the chart and the green lines show the baseline.

2 Starting at the center, work the **lion** using vanilla for the body, orange and sunflower for the mane, lilac for the ears and mouth, orange for the tail tip and nose, and turquoise for the eyes.

3 Work the other animals to the left of the lion in turn. Stitch the **hippo** in ice, outlined in turquoise with a dark-peach ear, and light mauve nostril and toes. Work the eye in black. The **jaguar** is outlined in caramel. Work orange for the body, brown for the markings and claws, and leave the face unstitched. Stitch two black eyes and nose. Finally, work the **camel** outline in caramel, the body in brown.

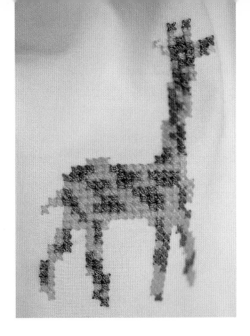

Simply by working the motif on two different fabrics, the look is transformed from subtly delicate (left) to homespun and chunky (far left).

Work a turquoise eye, a light-mauve nostril, and lilac feet.

4 To the right of the lion, work the **crocodile** outline in turquoise, the main body in pistachio with markings in grass, leave the teeth unstitched and work a lilac eye. The **elephant** is outlined in dark peach, filled in light mauve, with a vanilla ear and toes, and a grass eye; leave the tusks unstitched. Finally, work the **giraffe** in brown and caramel with lilac ears and nose, and a turquoise eye.

5 When the design is complete, remove the basting stitches and the waste canvas. Gently press on the reverse side of the embroidery.

How to work the blanket

1 Choose one of the motifs from the chart. Working from the corner of the blanket, identify a starting point for the motif. Work counted cross stitch so that each stitch on the chart corresponds with one knitted stitch on the blanket.

2 Personalize the blanket by adding a few letters or initials (see the chart on page 122).

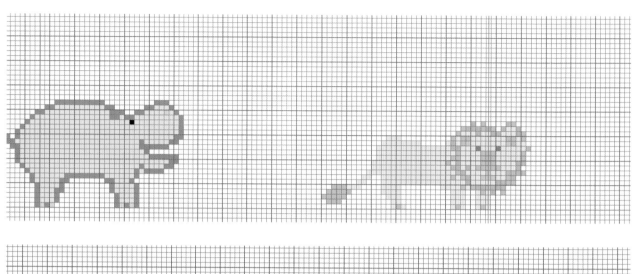

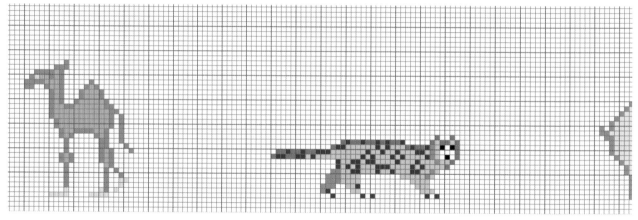

COLOR GUIDES

for lion	lilac 210	orange 742	turquoise 996	sunflower 3821	vanilla 3823
for hippo	ice 162	black 310	light mauve 778	turquoise 996	dark peach 3328
for jaguar	black 310	brown 433	orange 742	caramel 976	
for camel	lilac 210	brown 433	light mauve 778	caramel 976	turquoise 996

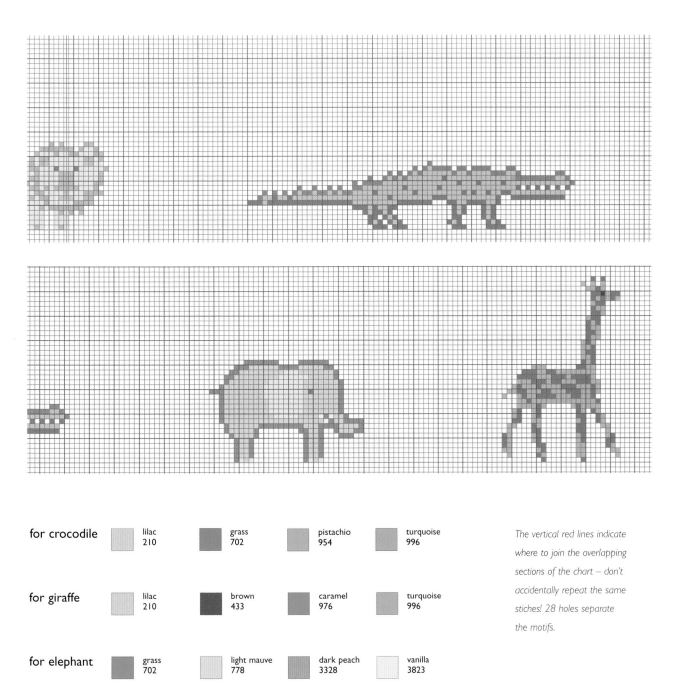

for crocodile		lilac 210		grass 702		pistachio 954		turquoise 996

for giraffe		lilac 210		brown 433		caramel 976		turquoise 996

for elephant		grass 702		light mauve 778		dark peach 3328		vanilla 3823

The vertical red lines indicate where to join the overlapping sections of the chart – don't accidentally repeat the same stiches! 28 holes separate the motifs.

how to make

BABY snuggle bag

I'm sure that sleeping in this cozy, comfy sleeping bag feels like drifting away in a cloud.

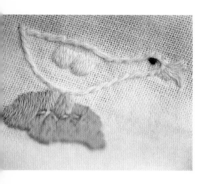

If ducks happen to be a favorite, then why not opt for a whole row of them quacking along.

FINISHED SIZE 16"x32" (40cmx80cm)

MATERIALS AND TOOLS

• DMC stranded embroidery cotton in the following shades:
  one skein of each color: **167** pale brown; **301** copper; **413** charcoal; **564** mint; **605** pink;
  726 lemon; **745** pale yellow; **746** cream; **747** baby blue; **3348** pale olive; **3713** light pink;
  3821 sunflower; **3823** vanilla

• 9"x17" (23cmx43cm) white cotton sheeting

• 17"x57" (43cmx145cm) polar fleece

• 17"x57"(43cmx145cm) 2oz iron-on batting (**Note:** health and safety guidelines for babies' bedding
  suggest that no more than a 2oz batting should be used)

• 17"x60½" (43cmx154cm) gingham fabric for the lining and edging strip

• 24" (60cm) zipper in a color to match the fleece

• Water-soluble marker

• Embroidery hoop

• Crewel needle, size 5

• Contrasting thread for basting

• Matching thread for sewing

TECHNIQUES A basic knowledge of either hand or machine sewing is needed. For all embroidery
techniques, see pages 114, 116–22.

STITCHES USED Chain stitch, French knot, lazy daisy stitch, running stitch, satin stitch, stem stitch,
and straight stitch

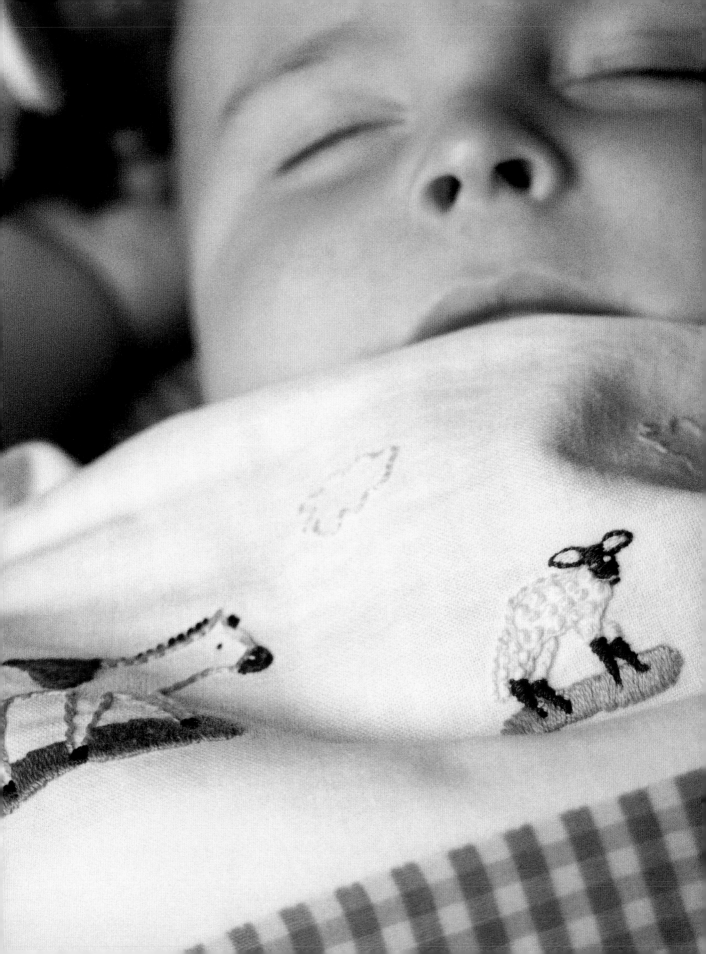

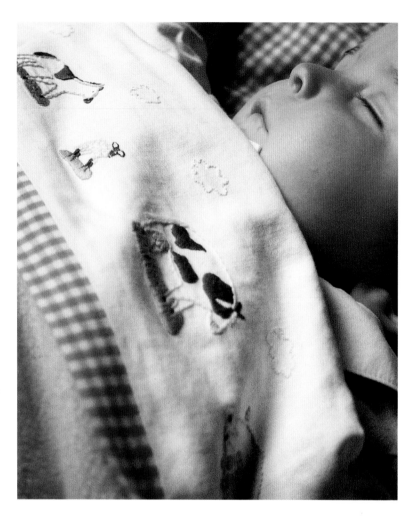

brown. For the nose ring, work a single lazy daisy stitch in pale yellow.

4 Outline the **horse** in split stitch in pale yellow. Work the saddle, grass, hooves, tail, and muzzle in satin stitch in pale olive, copper, and pale brown respectively. Stitch the mane in tiny straight stitches and the eye in French knots, both in pale brown.

5 Stitch the **lamb** outline in vanilla split stitch, filling in the fleece with random cream French knots. Work the grass in mint in satin stitch. Also in satin stitch, work the legs and face in charcoal and the ears in baby pink. Work the eyes in French knots in cream and the outline of the ears in split stitch in charcoal.

6 Outline the body of the **cow** in split stitch in cream and fill in the patches in copper. Work the udders and nose in baby pink, the grass in pale olive, the horns and hooves in pale brown, and the ears in cream – all in satin stitch. To complete the cow and using French knots, work the eye and nostril in charcoal and the teats in baby pink.

7 Work the **duck** outline and its wing in lemon, using stem and satin stitch respectively. Work the grass as before in mint and the eye in a single charcoal French knot. Stitch the legs and feet as straight stitches in sunflower.

8 The **sow** is lying on a bed of satin stitch straw worked in sunflower. Outline her body in stem stitch in baby pink. Work her ears, snout, and the piglets in satin stitch in pink and baby pink. Work chain stitch for the piglets' tails and tiny charcoal straight stitches for their feet.

9 Stitch the **clouds** in running stitch in baby blue and the **sun**, also in running stitch, in pale yellow.

These lively farm animals will quickly become familiar favorites to a small child.

Working the embroidery

1 Fold the sheeting panel in half lengthwise to find the center. Press the fold and then open the fabric out.

2 Enlarge the template to 200%. Transfer it, centered, onto the panel.

3 Working with three strands throughout and from left to right, work the outline of the **bull** in split stitch in charcoal. Work his ears, hooves, and tail in pale brown in satin stitch. Work his hair as a group of French knots in copper and his horns in satin stitch in cream. Work the grass in mint in satin stitch and the eyes and nostrils as tiny French knots in pale

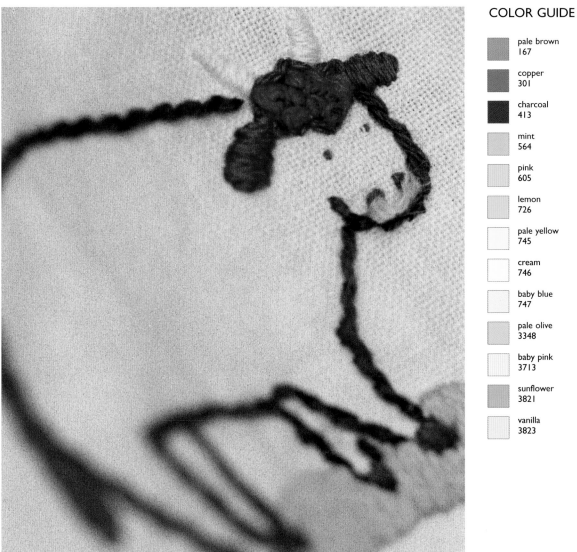

COLOR GUIDE

pale brown
167

copper
301

charcoal
413

mint
564

pink
605

lemon
726

pale yellow
745

cream
746

baby blue
747

pale olive
3348

baby pink
3713

sunflower
3821

vanilla
3823

TEMPLATE

grain of fabric

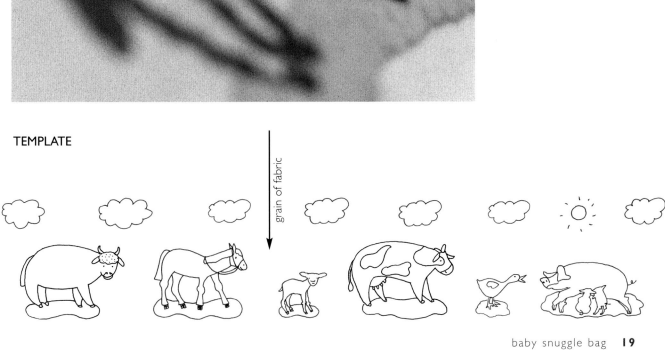

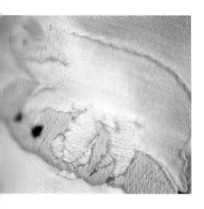

Textured stitches give the sow and her farmyard friends adorable appeal.

How to make your snuggle bag

1 Cut the fleece and batting panels to the sizes given in the materials list, which include a ⅝" (1.5cm) seam allowance all around.

2 Cut a 3½"×17" (9cm×43cm) strip from the width of the gingham fabric and press it in half lengthwise. This leaves a 17"×57" (43cm×145cm) piece of gingham.

3 With right sides facing, line up one long side of the gingham strip with the long raw edge under the embroidery on the sheeting. Sew along this edge, allowing a ⅝" (1.5cm) seam. Press the seam flat toward the gingham. Turn the gingham strip to the right side over the raw edge of the sheeting.

4 Pin the embroidered sheeting panel onto the fleece, right sides facing and 9" (23cm) down from the top edge of the fleece (see illustration below). Baste, then stitch the embroidered panel in place, allowing for a ⅝" (1.5cm)

seam. Turn the embroidered panel over, right side out, and smooth it onto the right side of the fleece, matching the remaining long raw edge of the panel with the top edge of the fleece. Press.

5 Iron the batting onto the wrong side of the gingham for the lining. Place the fleece with the embroidered panel on top of the lining and batting, right sides together, so that the batting makes the bottom layer.

6 Mark an opening, twice the length of the zipper, down one side of the fleece panel, starting at the top edge of the embroidered panel. Pin, baste, and machine stitch along both side edges of the fleece panel, leaving the zipper opening unstitched. Turn the fleece panel right side out.

7 Fold the fleece panel across its width, halfway along the zipper opening, to make the bag. Turn under a ⅝" (1.5cm) seam to the wrong

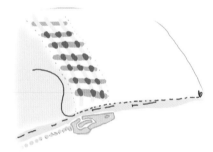

side along both edges of the zipper opening and press. Insert the zipper (see illustration at left), placing the bottom end of the zipper at the fold and the top end to the upper edge of the embroidered panel. Zip up the side.

8 Discreetly slip stitch the remaining side edge together. Remove any basting stitches

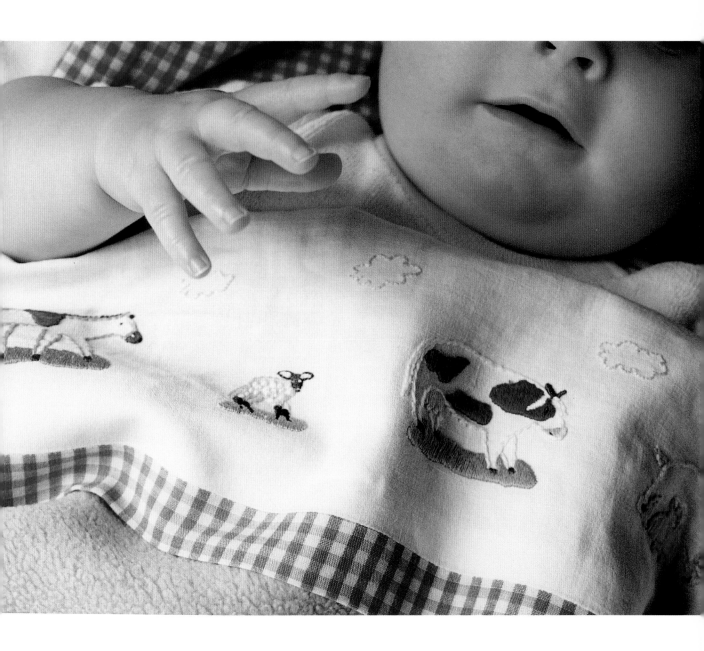

how to make
FARM-edged blanket

Yarn-edged blankets are a little too rough for a baby's delicate skin, so an embroidered edging is born of necessity as well as decoration.

The texture of pearl cotton gives the outline of each motif a three-dimensional quality.

FINISHED SIZE The width of the finished edging depends on the size of the blanket.

MATERIALS

- Two skeins of DMC pearl cotton no. 5 in **729** toffee
- Two skeins of DMC stranded embroidery cotton in **3821** sunflower
- Baby blanket
- 13¼" (33cm) length of white cotton sheeting, the width of the top edge of the baby blanket plus 1¼" (3cm)
- Dressmakers' ruler
- Dressmakers' pins
- Water-soluble marker
- Crewel needle, size 5
- Contrasting thread for basting
- Matching thread for sewing

TECHNIQUES A basic knowledge of either hand or machine sewing is needed. For all embroidery techniques, see pages 114, 116, 118, 119, and 121.

STITCHES USED Fern stitch, French knot, stem stitch

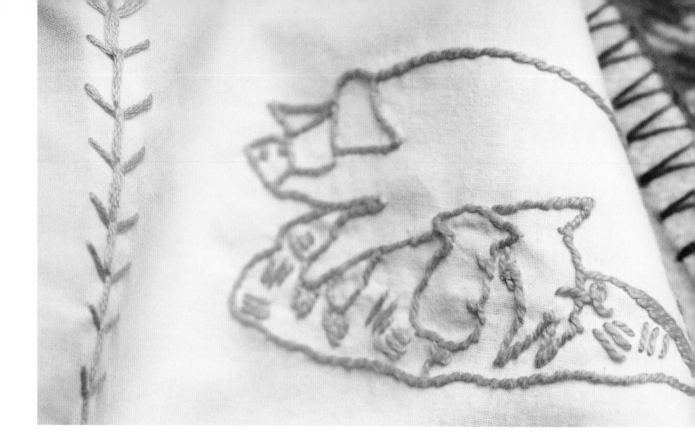

COLOR GUIDE

 toffee
729

 sunflower
3821

TEMPLATES

To begin the edging

1 Cut a strip of cotton sheeting to the same width as the top edge of the blanket 12" (30cm) deep, plus ⅝" (1.5cm) all around for seam allowances.

2 Enlarge the templates on a photocopier to 200% and loosely cut them out.

3 Plan out the placement of the animal motifs on the cotton sheeting, using the ruler to measure the gaps between them and dressmakers' pins for markers. Make sure the motifs are 18" (45cm) from the bottom raw edge and placed evenly across the width of the cotton sheeting.

4 Using the water-soluble marker, transfer the templates onto the cotton sheeting, using your pin markers as guides.

5 Using the set square and ruler, draw a vertical line with the water-soluble marker from the base edge to the top edge at each end of the cotton sheeting strip and between each of the motifs to divide them.

To work the embroidery

1 Embroider each motif in turn, working with the toffee pearl cotton.

2 Stitch each outline in stem stitch, carefully following the lines of the design as closely as the stitch allows.

3 Work any eyes or nostrils with one French knot each.

4 To finish the embroidery, work fern stitch along each of the ruled lines with four strands of sunflower in the needle (see illustration at right).

To make up the edged blanket

1 Press the border strip in half lengthwise, wrong sides facing. Press under a ⅝" (1.5cm) hem along one long edge of the strip.

2 Line up the raw edge of the strip along the top edge of the blanket, right side of the strip to the wrong side of the blanket. Sew a seam with a ⅝" (1.5cm) allowance.

3 Turn the border strip to the right side over the top edge of the blanket. Pin and slip stitch the hem of the border in place.

4 Turn in each end of the border by ⅝" (1.5cm) and slip stitch in place.

Fern stitch adds detail between the farmyard motifs that is both effective and easy to achieve.

Take your pick from this pair of cuddly friends and embroider a smiley face your child will come to know and love.

how to make
ANIMAL cuddlers

Lamby soft and huggably floppy, the happy smiley faces on these soft toys will be irresistible to your baby boy or girl.

FINISHED SIZE Each toy is approximately 12" (30cm) square.

MATERIALS AND TOOLS

• DMC stranded embroidery cotton in the following shades:
  one skein of each color: **monkey** – **435** toffee; **746** cream; **778** light mauve; **801** chocolate;
  lion – **435** toffee; **778** light mauve; **3816** jade; **3821** sunflower
• 6"×6" (15cm×15cm) plain white cotton flannel for each toy
• 20"×20" (50cm×50cm) patterned fabric of your choice for each toy
• 20"×20" (50cm×50cm) fleece fabric for each toy: cream for the monkey, yellow for the lion
• 5"×5" (14cm×14cm) fleece fabric in pink for the monkey
• Dressmakers' carbon paper
• Embroidery hoop
• Crewel needle, size 5 or 6
• Dressmakers' pins
• Contrasting thread for basting
• Matching thread for sewing
• Polyester fiberfill stuffing

TECHNIQUES A basic knowledge of either hand or machine sewing is needed. For all embroidery techniques, see pages 114, 116–22.

STITCHES USED Chain stitch, French knot, running stitch, split stitch, straight stitch

MONKEY TEMPLATES

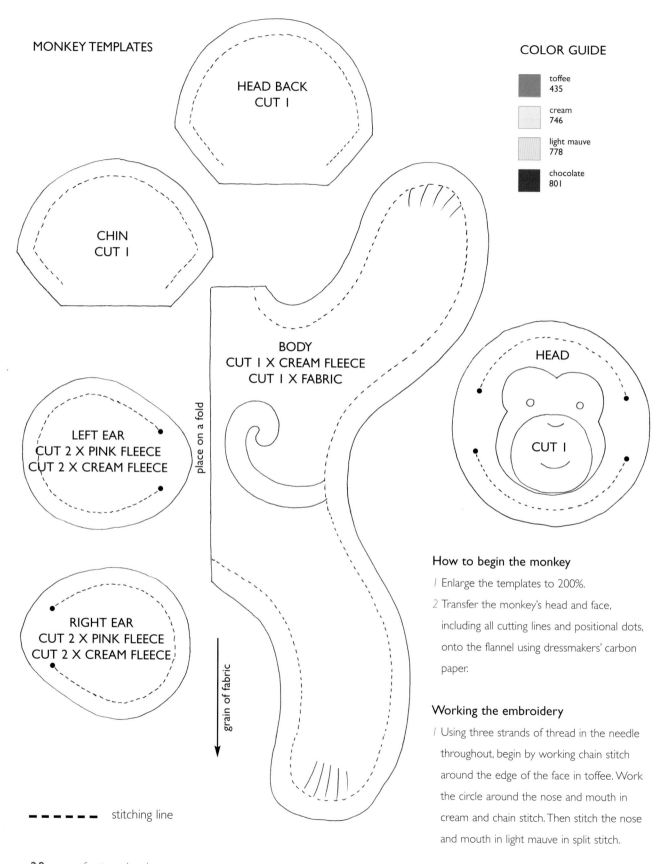

HEAD BACK
CUT 1

CHIN
CUT 1

BODY
CUT 1 X CREAM FLEECE
CUT 1 X FABRIC

place on a fold

LEFT EAR
CUT 2 X PINK FLEECE
CUT 2 X CREAM FLEECE

RIGHT EAR
CUT 2 X PINK FLEECE
CUT 2 X CREAM FLEECE

grain of fabric

HEAD
CUT 1

COLOR GUIDE

toffee
435

cream
746

light mauve
778

chocolate
801

- - - - - stitching line

How to begin the monkey

1 Enlarge the templates to 200%.

2 Transfer the monkey's head and face,
including all cutting lines and positional dots,
onto the flannel using dressmakers' carbon
paper.

Working the embroidery

1 Using three strands of thread in the needle
throughout, begin by working chain stitch
around the edge of the face in toffee. Work
the circle around the nose and mouth in
cream and chain stitch. Then stitch the nose
and mouth in light mauve in split stitch.

2 To complete the face, work each eye in chocolate straight stitches, radiating each stitch out from the center of the eye to the outer edge.

3 Cut out the head around the outer edge and put it to one side while you start the body.

4 Press the patterned fabric in half and, positioning the body pattern on the fold of the fabric, cut out one piece. Open the fabric out and press. Using the carbon paper, transfer the design for the tail and the feet.

5 Work the tail in chain stitch using toffee thread.

6 Use this body piece as a template for the fleece front. Pin it onto the fleece and then cut out around the outer edge.

7 Carefully cut out the paper templates for the head back, chin, and left and right ears to make a paper pattern of each. Pin the patterns to the fleece and cut out the required number of shapes as indicated on the templates, marking the positional dots with a stitch or two.

Making the monkey

1 Use a ⅜" (1cm) seam allowance throughout.

2 To stitch up the ears, place one right cream ear and one right pink ear right sides facing, matching the edges and dots. Sew around the edge of the ear, leaving an opening between the two dots. Turn it right side out through the opening. Do the same for the left ear.

3 To make the head, place the head back and chin pieces right sides facing and sew the three straight edges together, leaving the curved edge open. Fold down one of the curved edges away from the other one so that you make a circle.

4 With right sides facing, place the face down

onto the circle, aligning the ear dots with the face dots. Pin and baste the shapes together, then sew along the stitching lines, leaving the gaps between the dots for the ears. Remove the basting stitches. Turn the head right side out through one of the openings for the ears.

5 Insert the ears into the openings in the seams on each side of the head. Tuck in the raw edges on the head and slip stitch the ears firmly in position (see illustration at right).

6 Place the two body sections together with right sides facing. Pin, baste, and sew all around, leaving the neck open. Trim the edges as necessary and turn out the body through the opening. Stuff the body very loosely and slip stitch the opening closed.

7 To join the head to the body, slip stitch the long straight edge of the chin to the neck edge of the body.

8 To complete the monkey, work the finger and toe markings with long, individual straight stitches in toffee on both the top and underside of the body.

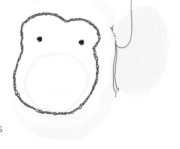

You could adapt this design to make other animal favorites, such as cats and dogs.

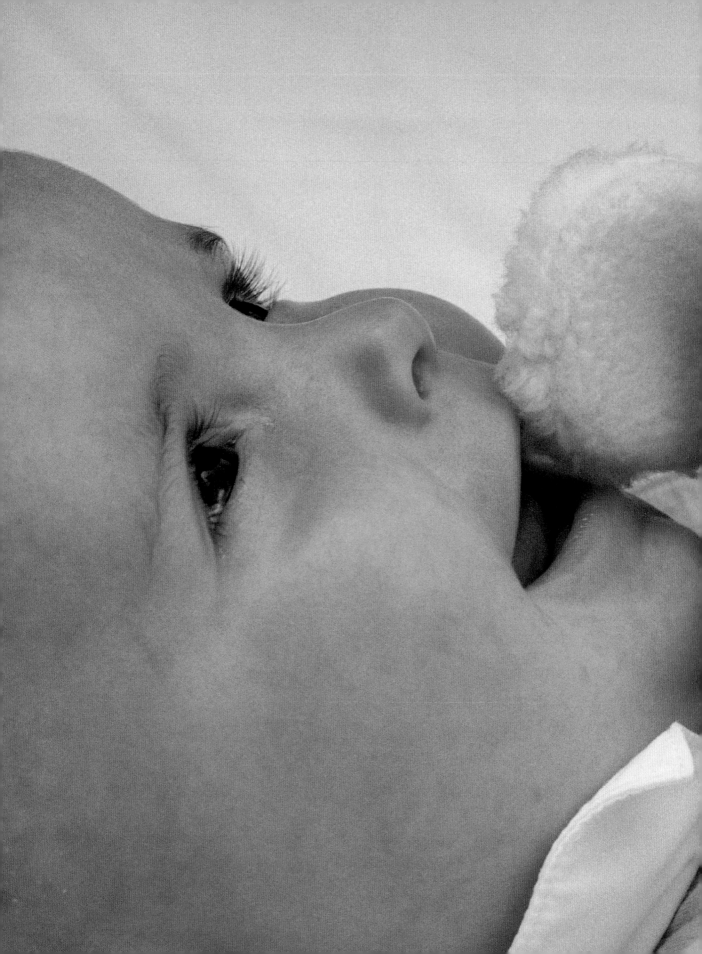

LION TEMPLATES

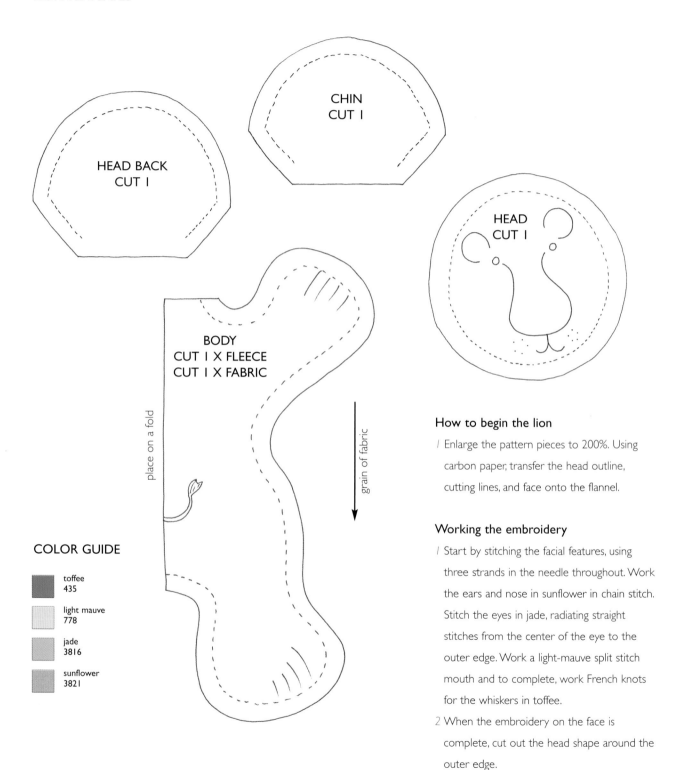

HEAD BACK
CUT 1

CHIN
CUT 1

HEAD
CUT 1

BODY
CUT 1 X FLEECE
CUT 1 X FABRIC

place on a fold

grain of fabric

COLOR GUIDE

toffee
435

light mauve
778

jade
3816

sunflower
3821

How to begin the lion

1 Enlarge the pattern pieces to 200%. Using carbon paper, transfer the head outline, cutting lines, and face onto the flannel.

Working the embroidery

1 Start by stitching the facial features, using three strands in the needle throughout. Work the ears and nose in sunflower in chain stitch. Stitch the eyes in jade, radiating straight stitches from the center of the eye to the outer edge. Work a light-mauve split stitch mouth and to complete, work French knots for the whiskers in toffee.

2 When the embroidery on the face is complete, cut out the head shape around the outer edge.

Making the lion

1 Press the patterned fabric in half and, positioning the body pattern on the fold of the fabric, cut out one piece. Open the fabric out and press. Using the carbon paper, transfer the design for the tail and claws.

2 Using toffee thread, work the tail in chain stitch and the tail tip in straight stitches.

3 Use this body piece as a template for the fleece front. Pin it onto the fleece and then cut it out around the outer edge.

4 Make paper pattern pieces for the chin and head back. Pin the patterns to the fleece and then cut out along the outer edges, marking the positional dots onto the fabric.

5 With right sides facing, lay the chin and head back pieces together, matching the dots and edges. Sew the two short straight seams, leaving the base edge open. Turn down one curved edge to create a circle.

6 Cut a 2¾"×12½" (7cm×31cm) strip of the patterned fabric for the mane. Sew the two short ends, right sides together, to make a ring of fabric. Press the seam open. Fold the fabric in half lengthwise, wrong sides facing, and press on the fold.

7 Work a gathering stitch by hand or machine ³⁄₁₆" (0.5cm) in from the long, raw edge. Pull the thread so the fabric gathers evenly until the ruffle measures the perimeter of the lion's face. Fit and pin the ruffle, aligning the edges and right sides together around the face shape. Tack to hold it in place (see illustration at right).

8 Lay the head back and chin circle on top of the face and ruffle, right sides facing. Pin, then baste. Allowing for a ³⁄₈" (1cm) seam, hand or machine sew around the circumference to join the three layers. Turn the head right side out through the opening at the neck. Remove any basting stitches.

9 To complete the lion, follow the directions in steps 7 and 8 for making up and finishing the embroidery on the monkey (page 29).

Sew up lion and monkey securely to withstand the rigors of being loved to bits.

how to make

SO-SOFT slippers

Handmade from natural fabrics with a so-soft fleece lining, these slippers make a perfectly cute gift for a baby shower.

These embroidered slippers are lined with fleece to keep tiny feet warm and cozy.

FINISHED SIZE To fit 3 to 6 months

MATERIALS AND TOOLS

- DMC stranded embroidery cotton in the following shades:
  one skein of each color – **433** brown; **746** cream; **747** baby blue; **761** salmon pink
- 5½"x9½" (14cmx24cm) linen fabric
- 5½"x9½" (14cmx24cm) colored fabric for the lining
- Two pieces of 2¾"x4⅜" (7cmx11cm) polar fleece for the soles
- Dressmakers' carbon paper
- Embroidery hoop
- Crewel needle, size 6
- Contrasting thread for basting
- Matching thread for sewing and buttons
- Dressmakers' pins
- 24"x⅝" in-wide (60cmx1.5cm-wide) cotton bias binding
- Two buttons, ⅜" (1cm) in diameter

TECHNIQUES A basic knowledge of either hand or machine sewing is needed. For all embroidery techniques, see pages 114, 116–22.

STITCHES USED Blanket stitch, chain stitch, French knot, running stitch, split stitch

TEMPLATES

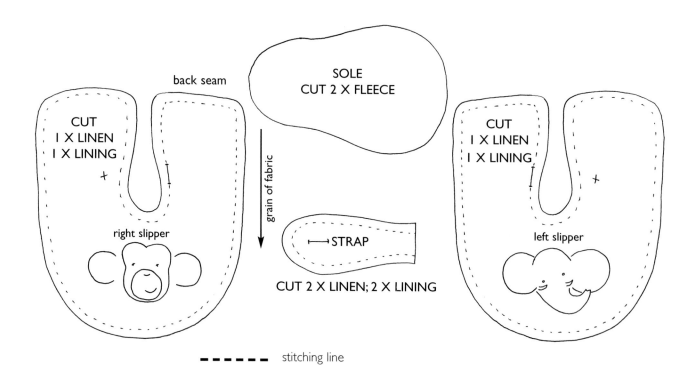

back seam

SOLE
CUT 2 X FLEECE

CUT
I X LINEN
I X LINING

＋

right slipper

grain of fabric

⊢—⊣ STRAP

CUT 2 X LINEN; 2 X LINING

CUT
I X LINEN
I X LINING

＋

left slipper

－ － － － － － stitching line

COLOR GUIDE

brown
433

cream
746

baby blue
747

salmon pink
761

How to begin the slippers

1 Enlarge the templates to 200%. Transfer the
motif and shoe patterns for each slipper onto
the linen fabric and the shoe pattern onto
the lining fabric. Do not cut them out yet.

2 Transfer the sole pattern onto the fleece
fabric to make two shapes. Cut them out.

Working the embroidery

1 Work the embroidery on the linen using two
strands of thread throughout.

2 To stitch the **monkey**, work around the
outline of the face in cream in chain stitch.

Embroider each ear outline in salmon
pink in chain stitch and around the nose
and mouth in split stitch in cream. Work a
salmon-pink split stitch nose and mouth. To
complete the monkey, stitch the eyes with
single French knots in brown.

3 To embroider the **elephant**, work chain stitch
along the top of the head and along the
trunk in baby blue. Outline the ears in
salmon pink in chain stitch and work the eyes
in brown single French knots. To complete,
work each tusk in cream, again in chain stitch.

You could also choose motifs from other projects in this book to decorate these slippers.

How to make up the slippers

1 Cut out the patterns for each slipper and strap. All the patterns allow for ³⁄₁₆" (0.5cm) seam allowances.

2 Match up the straps, cotton to linen, with wrong sides facing. Turn under ³⁄₁₆" (0.5cm) on both fabrics to the wrong sides almost all around, sandwiching in the raw ends. Leave the base edge of each strap open. Working in running stitch and matching thread, stitch close around the outside edge.

3 Mark and cut a buttonhole to fit the diameter of the button. Work the buttonhole in blanket stitch using matching thread to conceal the raw edges.

4 With right sides facing and a ³⁄₁₆" (0.5cm) seam allowance, stitch up the back seam of each linen slipper. Press the seams flat. Repeat for the linings.

5 Place the lining and linen wrong sides together, aligning the back seams. Turn under ³⁄₁₆" (0.5cm) on both fabrics to sandwich and conceal the raw edges. Baste, leaving an opening on each slipper for the strap.

6 Place the raw end of one of the straps between the linen and the lining of each slipper in the position marked on the pattern. Pin and baste it securely in place.

7 Work running stitch in matching thread close around the outside edges (see illustration at right).

8 Start at the back seam and join one long edge of the bias binding to the bottom edge of a slipper. When you reach the back again, cut the binding ³⁄₁₆" (0.5cm) longer than the edge. Fold in the raw end and stitch it neatly in place.

9 Pin and baste one of the soles to one of the slippers, with the wide part of the sole at the front. Baste the sole to the bottom edge of the slipper; then attach the bias binding to the sole with running stitch to hide the raw edges. Repeat steps 8 and 9 for the other slipper and then remove the pins and basting stitches. To complete, sew one button on each slipper, using the buttonholes as a guide.

CHAPTER TWO dream babies

Delicate designs, including airy fairies and fantastic unicorns in pastel hues of petal pink and baby goose-feather blues, set the perfect scene for a dreamy princess.

Dream

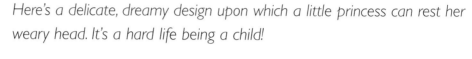

DREAMY fairies pillowcase and unicorn quilt

Here's a delicate, dreamy design upon which a little princess can rest her weary head. It's a hard life being a child!

The fairytale embroidery on this bed set will entice any little princess to a world of sweet dreams.

FINISHED SIZE **Pillowcase:** standard twin-sized pillowcase 20"x30" (48cmx75cm)

Quilt: 48"x56" (120cmx140cm)

MATERIALS AND TOOLS

• DMC stranded embroidery cotton in the following shades:

one skein in each color – **225** light shell pink; **422** fawn; **727** light lemon; **745** pale yellow; **828** ice blue; **893** bright pink; **963** baby pink; **3609** carnation; **3755** light smoke; **3821** sunflower

For the pillowcase

• Plain white cotton pillowcase

• 40" (1m) *broderie anglaise* or antique lace for the decorative border

For the quilt

• 21"x47" (53cmx120cm) plain white cotton sheeting for the embroidered panel

• 37"x47" (93cmx120cm) patterned fabric for the decorative border

• 48½"x56" (123cmx143cm) plain white sheeting for the backing fabric

• 47"x55" (120cmx140cm) 4oz batting (if the quilt is for a crib, use 2oz batting in accordance with health and safety guidelines for babies' bedding)

• 58" (146cm) strip of *broderie anglaise* or antique lace for the decorative edging

For both projects

• Dressmakers' carbon paper

• Embroidery hoop

• Crewel needle, size 6

• Dressmakers' pins

• Contrasting thread for basting

• Matching thread for sewing

TECHNIQUES For all embroidery techniques, see pages 114, 116, 120–22.

STITCHES USED Chain stitch, satin stitch, stem stitch

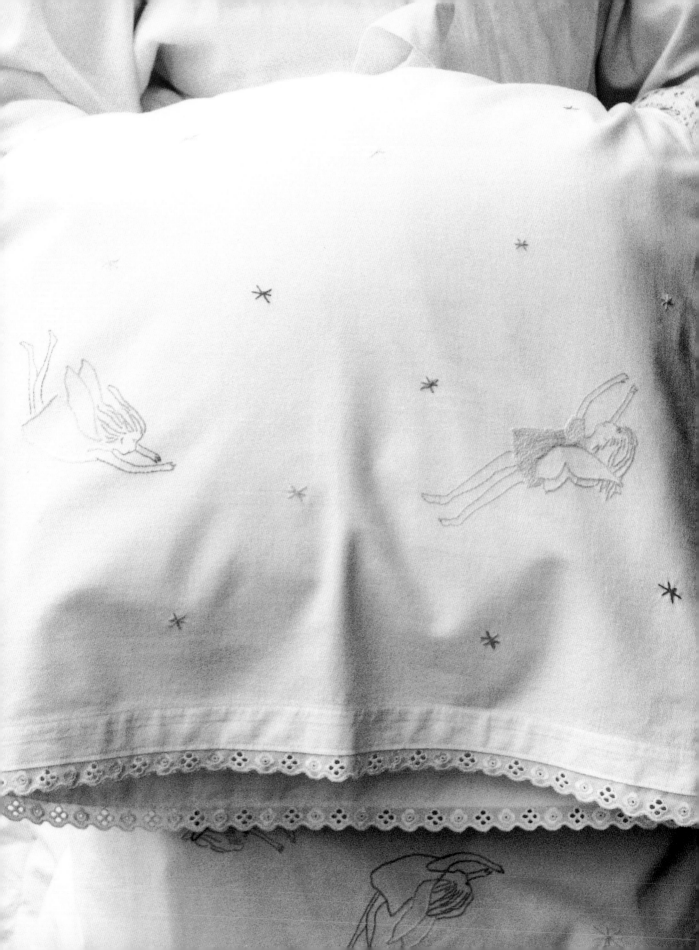

Each outline is worked in a palette of pastel shades and delicate stitches to enhance the airiness of the fairies.

To begin the pillowcase and quilt panel

1 Enlarge the templates to 200%. Then photocopy each motif and roughly cut around each one.

2 Arrange the motifs in a pleasing manner on the right side of the front of the pillowcase. Slipping the carbon paper shiny side down beneath each motif, transfer them into place. Remember to keep the motifs away from the edge of the pillowcase so that you can place the work easily in the hoop.

3 Using the same motifs, position them across the white sheeting for the quilt. Arrange the motifs in a balanced design, keeping them away from the edges as before.

Working the embroidery

1 Embroider the **bright pink fairy**. With one strand of fawn thread, work around the outline of the face (including the ear and mouth), arms, and legs in stem stitch, keeping as close to the design line as possible.

2 Work the hair in two strands of light lemon in split stitch. Work the wings in split stitch, this time with two strands in ice blue. Continuing with the same color, work two straight stitches to make the eye. Finally, using two strands of bright pink, work chain stitch around the outline of the dress.

3 For the **baby pink fairy**, take one strand of the light shell pink thread and work around

TEMPLATES

Baby pink fairy

Bright pink fairy

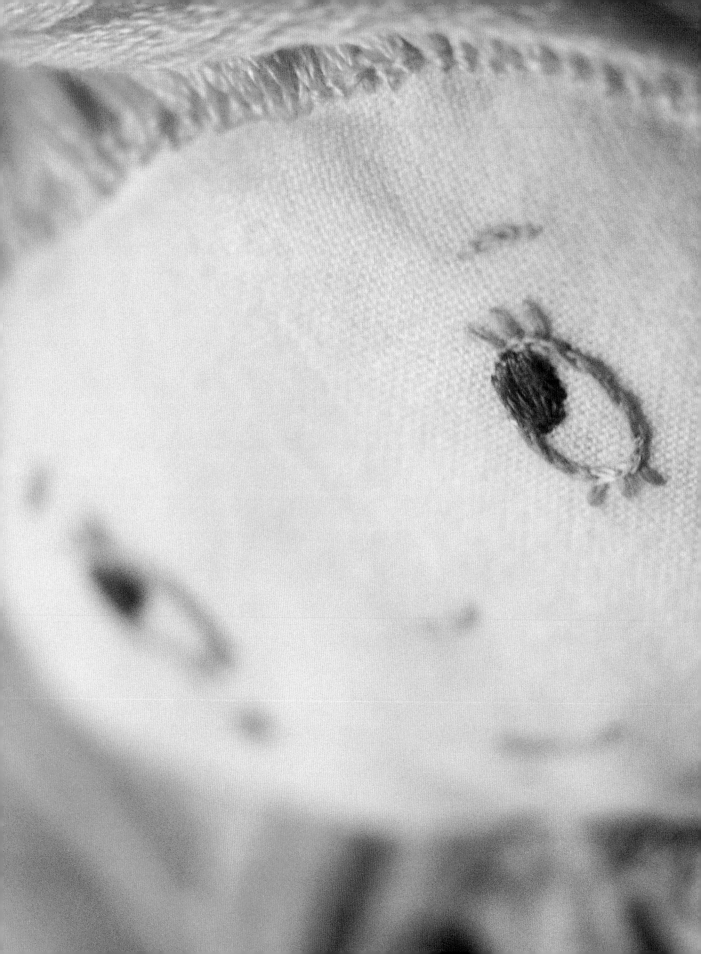

To begin the doll

1 Cut an 8" (20cm) square out of the white cotton sheeting.

2 Enlarge the face template on page 56 to 200%. Transfer the outlines for the face, eyes, nose, mouth, and cheeks directly onto the fabric, using the water-soluble marker.

Working the embroidery

1 Working with two strands of thread in the needle throughout, begin by stitching each eye iris with dark smoke in satin stitch. In split stitch and with light smoke, work an outline almost all around the eye (refer to the photograph at left).

2 With the pale-yellow thread, work three straight stitches above and below each eye to make the eyelashes. With the same color, work two split stitch eyebrows.

3 Embroider a split stitch nose in light shell pink. Then use bubblegum pink to work a split stitch mouth and two satin stitch cheeks.

4 Cut another 8" (20cm) square from the cotton sheeting for the back of the head. Lay it onto the embroidered square, right sides facing, edges matching. Pin, baste, and sew them together along the stitching line, leaving an opening at the base of the neck.

5 Cut around the head along the heavy outer line. Turn the head right side out through the neck opening and lightly stuff with fiberfill stuffing. Slip stitch the opening to close.

6 The hairline is made up of two rows of single looped strands of thread. Cut the pale-yellow thread into 16" (40cm) lengths. Then separate the strands in each length into pairs.

7 Begin attaching the hair by folding one pair of strands in half and threading the unfolded

raw ends through the needle. Then, with the face on top and starting above one of the ears, insert the needle into the seam around the head. Push the needle out a tiny distance along the seam from where it was initially inserted. As the needle emerges, place the looped end of the thread over the needle point. Pull the thread taut until the loop lies on the seam at the top of the head (see illustrations on page 91). Continue in this way along the seam to the other ear, working the looped stitches as close to each other as you can.

Making the doll's body

1 Enlarge the templates for the body, arms, and legs by 200%. Transfer the templates onto the white sheeting and cut out the required number of pieces.

2 Open out the two arm sections, place them together, and sew around the seam line, leaving an opening of about 1¼" (3cm) in the middle. Turn the arms right side out through the opening.

3 Stuff the hands and the arms using the poly pellets for about 6" (15cm) up each arm, then plug up to 2½" (6cm) of toy stuffing on top to retain the granules. You should now have an unstuffed section between the two arms, which will eventually be inserted into the body cavity.

4 Sew up each leg, leaving the top ends open for turning. Turn the legs right side out through the opening. Stuff each leg with poly pellets up to the knee and then complete the stuffing with the fiberfill. Leave ⅝" (1.5cm) from the top unstuffed, for sewing into the body.

Position the pupils in the eyes of this doll with care — her upturned gaze looks particularly winsome and appealing.

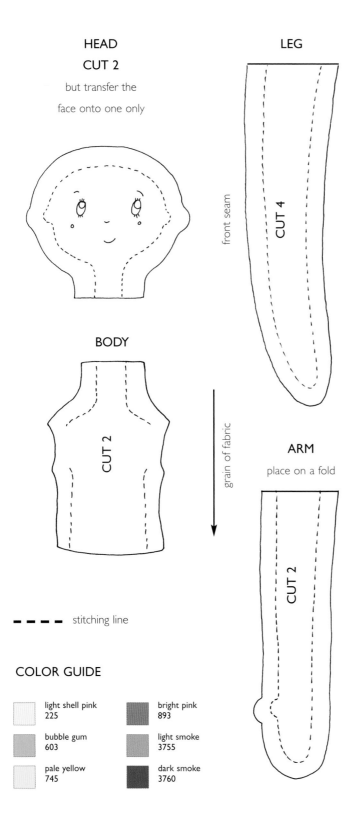

HEAD
CUT 2

but transfer the
face onto one only

BODY

CUT 2

grain of fabric

LEG

front seam

CUT 4

ARM

place on a fold

CUT 2

- - - - stitching line

COLOR GUIDE

light shell pink
225

bright pink
893

bubble gum
603

light smoke
3755

pale yellow
745

dark smoke
3760

5 Place the body sections together. Sew along the seam lines, leaving openings at the neck, armholes, and base. Turn the body right side out and tuck in the raw edges.

6 Thread the arms through the arm opening. Make sure both arms are of even length and that any raw edges are concealed. Then oversew neatly to secure the arms in place.

7 Insert the legs into the opening at the base of the body. Check that both legs are level and that the front seam lies facing you. Oversew the legs securely in place.

8 Work toy stuffing into the body through the neck opening. Insert the neck into the opening, leaving about ⅛" (3mm) showing, and oversew to secure the head. To remove the lines made with the marker, just dampen with a sponge.

To make the doll's dress

1 Enlarge the template for the dress to 200%. Fold the dress fabric in half, right sides facing, and press. Place the template against the fold of the fabric, draw around it, and then mark off the shoulder points. Cut out two pieces.

2 Open the dress fabric out, press it, and place the back and front together, right sides facing. Sew from the shoulder to the armhole and down the side seams, with a ⅜" (1cm) seam allowance and leaving openings at the neck, and the arm and base hemlines. Clip into the angle under the arms and oversew to secure the seam.

3 Fold under a 3/16" (0.5cm) hem to the wrong side around the neck opening. Using a contrasting thread and two strands of thread, work running stitch close to the edge. Don't secure the thread at each end, but leave a tail

Attach the ruffle to the dress with contrasting thread to give an extra level of detail.

of about 2½" (6cm), as the neck will be gathered up when the doll is dressed.

4 Work a similar gathering stitch around the waistline, and also halfway up both sleeves, leaving the threads loose as before.

5 At the cuffs, turn under a ³⁄₁₆" (0.5cm) hem to the wrong side and press. Attach a piece of antique lace to each hem, sewing it in place with white cotton thread.

6 Cut a 29"×4" (74cm×10cm) piece of checked fabric for the ruffle. Sew a ³⁄₁₆" (0.5cm) hem along the two short edges. Fold the ruffle in half along the length, wrong sides facing, and press. Sew a hand or machine gathering stitch ³⁄₁₆" (0.5cm) from the top raw edge.

7 Fold under a ³⁄₁₆" (0.5cm) hem to the wrong side on the lower edge of the dress. Gather up the ruffle to the same length as the dress hem. Pin and tack it into position. With two strands of contrasting thread (such as bright pink), work a running stitch close to the hemmed edge to attach the ruffle (see photograph above).

8 Dress the doll and gather up the threads around the body and arms. Tie them in place.

TEMPLATE

DRESS

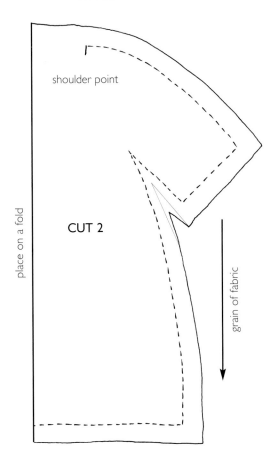

shoulder point

place on a fold

CUT 2

grain of fabric

how to make

DOLLY'S quilt

Scraps of cotton fabric are an excellent choice for this quilt, which will be so indispensable that it will need frequent washing!

A thrifty and attractive essential for little girls, this quilt is a good way of using up scraps of favorite old fabrics. It can be made even more original with sampler-type letters and motifs, perhaps with the child's initials or even the doll's name. Of course, the more ambitious could turn a miniature dolly's quilt into a full-sized family heirloom.

FINISHED SIZE Approximately 15"×19" (38cm×48cm)

MATERIALS AND TOOLS

- DMC stranded embroidery cotton in shades to match or contrast with the color theme of the quilt; one letter takes about half a skein
- Remnants and scraps of patterned, plain, and floral cotton fabric; the maximum size needed is 4"×4" (10cm×10cm)
- 4"×4" (10cm×10cm) waste canvas × the number of embroidered hexagons
- 16"×20" (41cm×51cm) cotton fabric for the backing (you could use an old pillowcase)
- Embroidery hoop
- Crewel needle, size 4, 5, or 6
- Small scraps of paper for paper templates
- Ruler and water-soluble marker
- Contrasting thread for basting
- Matching thread for sewing

TECHNIQUES A basic knowledge of either hand or machine sewing is needed. For all embroidery techniques, see pages 114 and 118. For using waste canvas and reading the chart, see page 115. For the alphabet chart, see page 122.

STITCHES USED Counted cross stitch

Working the embroidery

1 Sew waste canvas onto the required number of plain cotton scraps, aligning it centrally and with the grain of the fabric. Decide on the letters and/or motifs you wish to embroider.

2 Using two strands of thread in colors of your choice, work counted cross stitch by following the alphabet chart on page 122.

3 When the embroidery is complete, strip out the waste canvas.

Making the quilt

1 Using the template as a guide to trace around, cut out 39 paper hexagons.

2 Cut out 39 fabric hexagons by tracing the template and then adding a $\frac{3}{8}$" (1cm) allowance all around. Make sure that any motif is centered and that one side of the hexagon is lined up against the grain of the fabric.

TEMPLATE

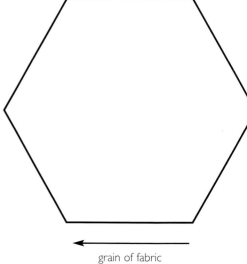

grain of fabric

3 Center one of the backing papers on the wrong side of one of the fabric pieces. Baste the paper onto the fabric. Turn in and press the ⅜" (1cm) allowance against the backing paper. Then baste the edges down, sewing through the paper (see illustration at top right). Repeat on all the fabric pieces.

4 Plan the placing of the hexagons, 6 across and 7 down, and mark a number on the back of each one in pencil to note their order.

5 To join two hexagons, lay them right sides together and line up the edges. Overstitch by hand along one edge. Sew through the fold of the fabric but try not to catch the paper. Press the seam open.

6 Join a third hexagon by oversewing one edge of the new shape to one edge of the original pair, adjacent to the existing seam. Open the seam out. Reposition the third hexagon to match the next edge with the appropriate one on the second hexagon (see illustration at bottom right). Oversew the edges and then press the seams open.

7 Continue in the same way until all 39 hexagons have been sewn in place. Remove the basting and the backing papers.

To make up the quilt

1 When the patchwork is complete, lay the backing fabric on top, edges matching and right sides together. Press out all the raw edges around the edges of the patchwork.

2 Machine stitch all around the quilt, allowing for a ⅜" (1cm) seam and leaving a 4" (10cm) opening on the bottom edge.

3 Turn the quilt right side out and slip stitch the opening closed. Press gently .

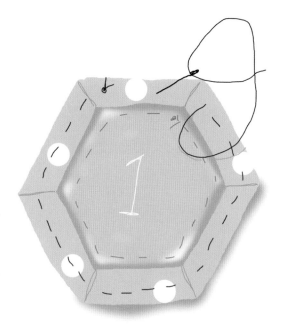

Use a collection of favorite fabrics that may have special memories attached, such as baby's first dress or a cherished, shabby old cushion. Be brave with your colors – after all, children adore anything bold and bright.

 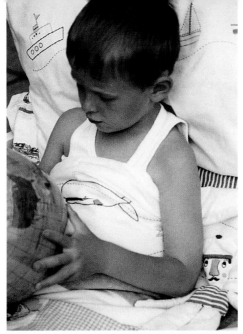 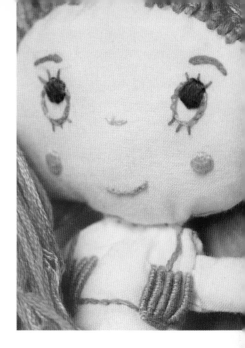

CHAPTER THREE adventurous spirits

Children wake up each day to a new adventure, a day that lasts forever in their eyes. The starring characters in this chapter will inspire creativity and stimulate the imagination to make that "endless day" last even longer!

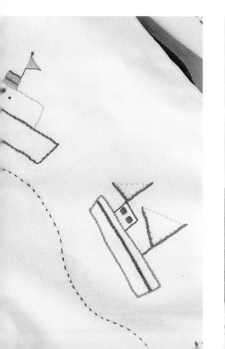  

how to make
WHALEY the whale

Old denim jeans, softened by years of washing, make an unusual soft toy and a perfect fabric for dear old Whaley.

Floppy and friendly, old jeans give Whaley that well-worn and lived-in look.

FINISHED SIZE 8¾" (22cm) high × 14½" (37cm) long

MATERIALS AND TOOLS

• DMC stranded embroidery cotton in the following shades:
  half a skein of each color – **210** lilac; **310** black; **B5200** white
• Scraps of denim fabric recycled from old jeans or shirts
• Scrap of blue fabric for the spout
• Dressmakers' carbon paper
• Embroidery hoop
• Polyester fiberfill stuffing
• Crewel needle, size 5 or 6
• Dressmakers' pins
• Contrasting thread for basting
• Matching thread for sewing
• Tailors' chalk

TECHNIQUES A basic knowledge of hand or machine sewing is needed. For all embroidery techniques, see pages 114, 116, 120–22.

STITCHES USED Chain stitch, satin stitch, stem stitch

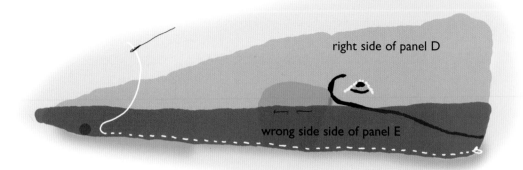

right side of panel D

wrong side side of panel E

To begin the whale

1 Enlarge the templates on a photocopier to 200%.

2 Make paper templates of all the sections, marking all the positional dots clearly.

3 With the tailors' chalk, draw around each template onto the denim and blue fabric to make the required number of shapes. Cut them out and open out the folded pieces.

4 Use the carbon paper to transfer the face markings onto each of the two sides of the whale top, shape D.

Working the embroidery

1 Using three strands of black thread, work the mouth in chain stitch on both D shapes.

2 Finish the embroidery in two strands. Work chain stitch in white along the top of the eye. Fill in the bottom half of the eye with lilac and the pupil in black, both in satin stitch. To complete the face, work the line underneath the eye in black stem stitch.

Making the whale

1 Place two tail pieces, shape A, right sides facing. Sew them together, allowing for a ⅜" (1cm) seam and leaving a 1¼" (3cm) opening at the base of the tail. Turn the tail right side out. Stuff it with polyester fiberfill and oversew the opening to close.

2 Lay the two pieces of blue fabric for the water spout, shape B, right sides facing.

TEMPLATES

- - - - stitching line

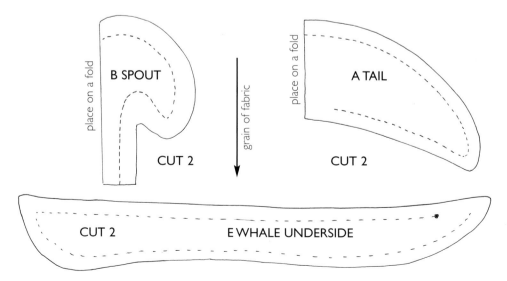

place on a fold

B SPOUT

grain of fabric

place on a fold

A TAIL

CUT 2

CUT 2

CUT 2   **E WHALE UNDERSIDE**

Sew around the shape with a ⅜" (1cm) seam, leaving the base edge open. Turn the water spout right way out and stuff it. Close the opening with a few stitches.

3 Place two pieces of fabric right sides together for each fin, shape C. Sew each fin with a ⅜" (0.5cm) seam allowance, leaving the flat edge open. Turn the fins right side out and press them flat.

4 Put one section D and the corresponding section E right sides together, aligning the joining edge. Slip one of the fins in place and then pin and tack the seam together. Sew along the seam, with a ⅜" (1cm) allowance, up to the dot at the tail end (see illustration at top left). Remove the basting stitches and repeat for the other side.

5 Lay the two parts of the whale's body right sides facing, making sure that the mouth will meet at the front seam. Slip the water spout in place and pin and baste all around. Hand or machine sew along the seam line with a ⅜" (1cm) allowance. Turn the body right side out.

6 Turn in a ⅜" (1cm) hem at the tail end of the body and press to hold. Stuff the body.

7 Slot the tail into the end of the body. Pin and tack it into position. Then carefully sew it in place with invisible stitches.

grain of fabric

CUT 4

C FIN

COLOR GUIDE

white
B5200

lilac
210

black
310

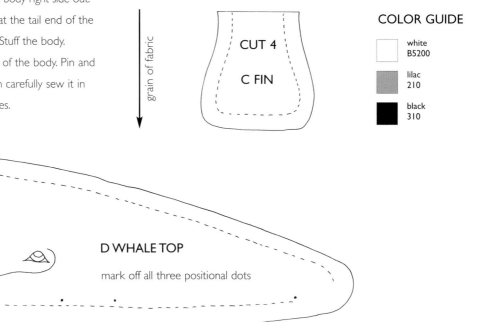

CUT 2

D WHALE TOP

mark off all three positional dots

how to make

BOBBING boats sheet

*A colorful flotilla of boats bobs jauntily along a crisp white cotton ocean.
This cheery design is reminiscent of halcyon days spent at the beach.*

*Use the motifs to decorate your own
buttons and add special detail to
clothes or bedding. Work the buttons in
chain stitch or satin stitch.*

FINISHED SIZE Twin or crib sheet size

MATERIALS AND TOOLS

- DMC stranded embroidery cotton in the following shades:
  one skein of each color – **309** raspberry; **349** red; **680** coffee; **727** light lemon; **801** chocolate;
  954 pistachio; **996** turquoise; **3609** carnation; **3755** light smoke; **3816** jade; **3821** sunflower;
  B5200 white

- Twin or crib sheet

- Length of blue rickrack measuring the width of the sheet (optional)

- Water-soluble marker

- Ruler

- Embroidery hoop

- Crewel needle, size 6

- Button covering kit for the required number of buttons

- Fabric scraps for buttons

TECHNIQUES For all embroidery techniques, see pages 114, 116–22.

STITCHES USED Chain stitch, French knot, running stitch, satin stitch, straight stitch

Mix and match the colors of thread to create a very individual flotilla of boats.

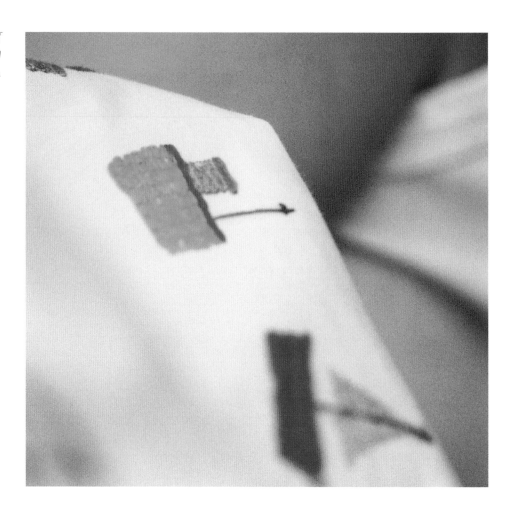

To begin the sheet

1 Draw a ruled line with a water-soluble marker 4" (10cm) from the short edge of the sheet along which you want to embroider the bobbing boats border.

2 Fold the fabric in half widthwise to find the center of the border line.

3 Photocopy the template. Align the red guideline on the template with the ruled line on the sheet. Starting on one side of the center fold and using the water-soluble marker, trace over the template directly onto the fabric. Repeat the design along the line to each edge of the sheet.

TEMPLATE

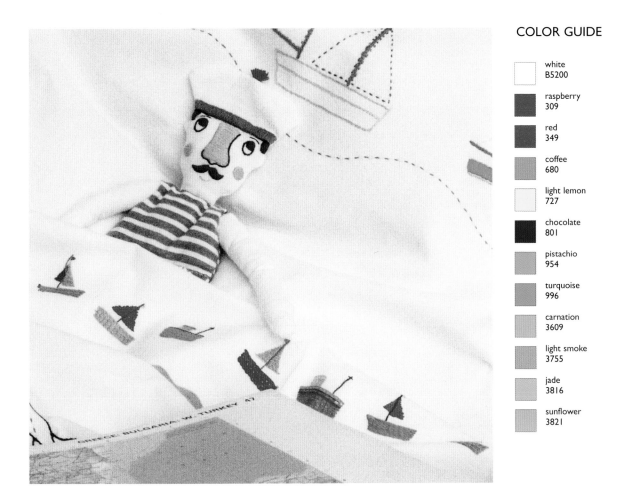

⬜	white B5200
🟪	raspberry 309
🟥	red 349
⬜	coffee 680
⬜	light lemon 727
⬛	chocolate 801
⬜	pistachio 954
🟦	turquoise 996
⬜	carnation 3609
⬜	light smoke 3755
⬜	jade 3816
⬜	sunflower 3821

Working the embroidery

1 Refer to the photographs for color usage or pick your own colors. Work the entire design with two strands in the needle.

2 For all boat hulls, cabins, and sails, work rows of chain stitch, keeping the rows close together to create a blocked area of solid color.

3 Work each of the masts in straight stitch and the flags in satin stitch.

4 Work the buoys as French knots and the windows in tiny individual running stitches.

5 As an optional extra detail, pin a length of blue rickrack about ⅜" (1cm) beneath the boats and sew it in place. Remove the pins.

How to work the buttons

1 Reduce one of the boat templates to fit the button pattern that appears on the reverse of the button-making kit.

2 Transfer the boat template onto a scrap of fabric, leaving enough fabric around the motif to fit around the button.

3 Embroider the boat in colors of your choice.

4 Make up the button according to the instructions on the kit.

5 Make the required number of buttons and sew them, for example, to the opening of a duvet cover.

how to make
BOATY pillowcase

Embroidery on fresh, crisp cotton makes the perfect pillowcase to settle down on and dream the night away.

Ship ahoy! Any child would want to sail off on an adventure with his head on this crisp pillow. "Hoist the main sail, me hearty!"

FINISHED SIZE 30"x20" (75cmx50cm) twin pillowcase size

MATERIALS AND TOOLS
- DMC stranded embroidery cotton in the following shades:
  one skein of each color – **349** red; **605** light cranberry; **680** coffee; **796** royal blue; **809** sky; **964** mint; **3817** pale leaf; **3821** sunflower
- 48"x48" (120cmx120cm) white cotton sheeting
- Dressmakers' ruler
- Water-soluble marker
- Embroidery hoop
- Crewel needle, size 6
- Dressmakers' pins
- Matching thread for sewing

TECHNIQUES A basic knowledge of either hand or machine sewing is needed. For all embroidery techniques, see pages 114, 116, 118–22.

STITCHES USED Chain stitch, running stitch, satin stitch, stem stitch, straight stitch

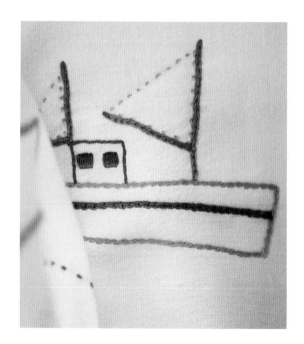

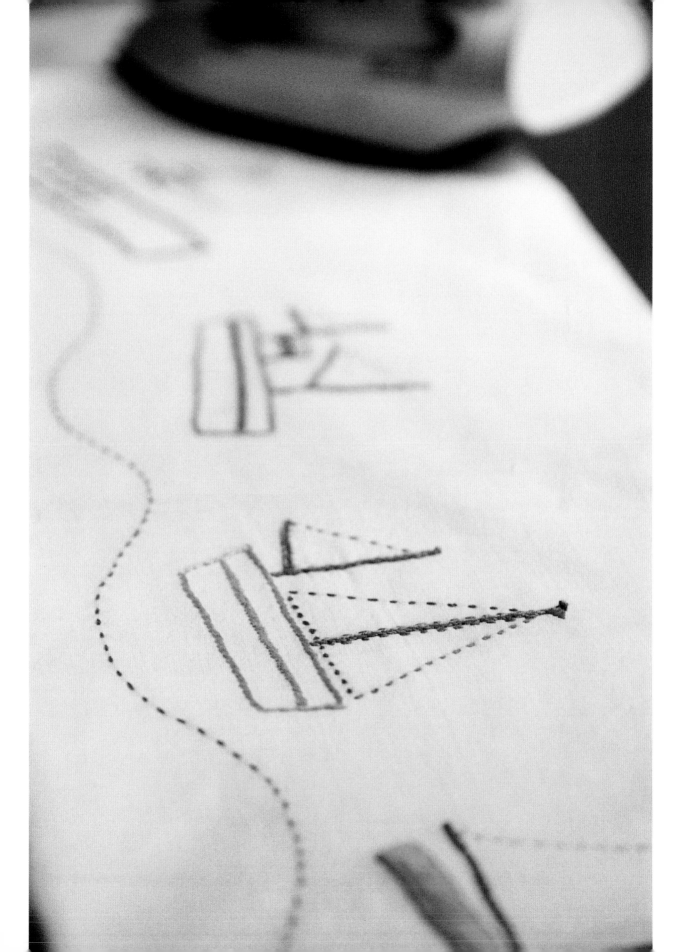

To begin the pillowcase

1 Cut the square of white cotton in half. Use the dressmakers' ruler to mark out a 31"x21" (79cmx54cm) rectangle on one piece of cotton and a 36"x21" (91cmx54cm) rectangle on the other. Cut them out.

2 Fold the shorter rectangle in half lengthwise and press. Then fold it widthwise and press to find the center point.

3 Enlarge the template to 200% and join the two sections by matching up the red crosses. Using the water-soluble marker, trace the design onto the fabric, placing the red cross on the template on the center point on the fabric.

Working the embroidery

1 Stitch the entire design with three strands of thread. Finish each boat before going on to the next, working from left to right.

2 Work the hull of **boat 1** in royal blue using stem stitch, and the portholes in tiny straight stitches in sky thread. Red French knots add to the detail of the cabin, which is outlined in light-cranberry stem stitch. Work the funnel in two rows of sky satin stitch, separated across the middle with a line of royal-blue stem stitch, topped with a coffee stem stitch

line. Work the mast in coffee stem stitch and the flag in pale-leaf satin stitch.

3 **Boat 2**'s sunflower hull is outlined using stem stitch with a line detail across the middle in royal-blue chain stitch. Outline the cabin using three rows of running stitch in red. Work the royal-blue windows in satin stitch and the masts in coffee chain stitch. To complete this boat, work the sails in tiny running stitches in sky thread.

4 Embroider the same stitches on **boat 3** as for boat 2, but use the following colors: a mint hull with light-cranberry linear detail, masts as boat 2 with a royal blue main sail and sunflower half sail. Finish with a red flag in satin stitch.

5 Work the hull of **boat 4** in satin stitch and sunflower thread. On the base of the hull, work a row in sky stem stitch; on the top, work a row of mint running stitch. Stitch the rigging in coffee stem stitch. Finish with a royal-blue flag in satin stitch atop the mast, a light-cranberry main sail and red half sail.

6 To complete the design, work the wavy line beneath the boats in a neat row of royal-blue running stitch. Gently press the embroidery from the back of the sheeting.

Match up the crosses on the wave line to join the two parts of the template.

TEMPLATE

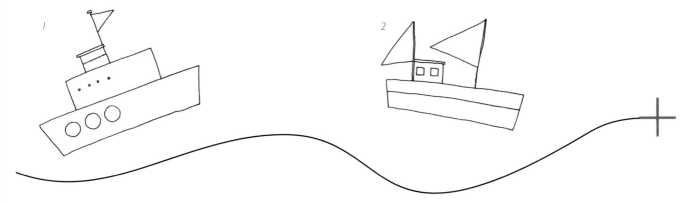

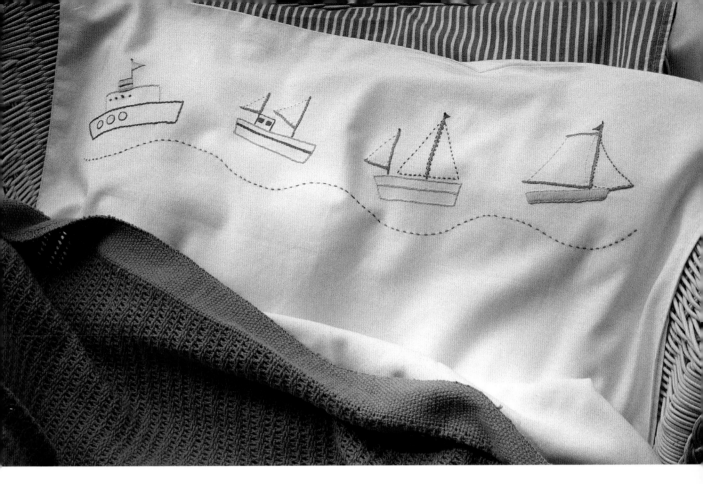

To make up the pillowcase

1 Turn a double ⅜" (1cm) hem to the wrong side across one of the short ends of the embroidered panel. Press and stitch in place.

2 Make a similar double hem along one short end of the other piece of fabric. Turn a 4¾" (12cm) flap to the wrong side and press.

3 Place the embroidered panel on top of the plain one, right sides together and aligning the unhemmed short ends. Fold the flap over to the wrong side of the embroidered piece.

4 Sew around all the three raw edges with a ¾" (2cm) seam allowance. Turn out the pillowcase through the opening and press.

COLOR GUIDE

red
349

light cranberry
605

coffee
680

royal blue
796

sky
809

mint
964

sunflower
3821

pale leaf
3817

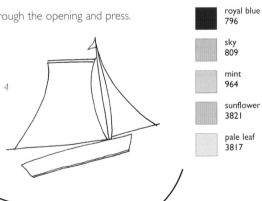

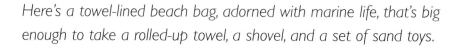

how to make
WHALES AND DOLPHINS
beach bag

Here's a towel-lined beach bag, adorned with marine life, that's big enough to take a rolled-up towel, a shovel, and a set of sand toys.

FINISHED SIZE 12"x18¼" (30cmx46.5cm)

MATERIALS AND TOOLS

- DMC stranded embroidery cotton in the following shades:

  one skein of each color – **317** gray; **387** ivory; **996** turquoise; **3078** primrose; **3760** dark smoke; **3816** jade; **3821** sunflower; **3843** medium blue

- 13"x33" (33cmx84cm) white cotton sheeting
- 13"x40" (33cmx100cm) white towelling
- 4¾"x26" (12cmx66cm) polka-dot fabric for the top edge
- 40"x³⁄₁₆" wide (1mx0.5cm wide) piping cord
- Masking tape
- Water-soluble marker
- Embroidery hoop
- Crewel needle, size 7
- Dressmakers' pins
- Contrasting thread for basting
- Matching thread for sewing

TECHNIQUES A basic knowledge of either hand or machine sewing is needed. For all embroidery techniques, see pages 114, 116–22.

STITCHES USED Chain stitch, French knot, running stitch, satin stitch, seed stitch, stem stitch

Various stitches are worked around the outlines to create a feeling of movement for this unique marine design.

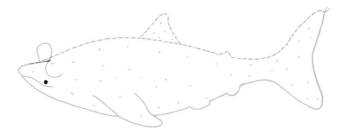

To begin the whale bag

1 Fold and press the cotton sheeting in half widthwise. Enlarge the templates on pages 80–81 on a photocopier to 200%.

2 Cut roughly around the paper templates and arrange over the bottom half of the cotton sheeting, taking care to get a good balance of shapes and making sure to leave a ⅝" (1.5cm) seam allowance.

3 When you are happy with the design, tape the templates in place if necessary. Then carefully smooth out the other half of the sheeting over the top so as not to disturb the templates beneath. Trace over the motifs with the water-soluble marker. Open out the fabric and remove the paper templates.

Working the embroidery

1 Embroider the motifs one at a time, referring to the photographs for color usage or picking your own colors for the different shapes.

2 Use three strands of thread for all the embroidery. Work the outlines of the fish in running, stem, or chain stitch. Embroider all the dots and eyes in single French knots, then work the short dashes in seed stitch, and the longer dashes in running stitch. Fill in small enclosed sections such as the fins in satin stitch or, for more texture and interest, in a combination of French knots, seed stitch, or chain stitch.

Making the whale bag

1 Fold the polka-dot fabric in half lengthwise and cut along the fold to make two strips of equal length.

2 Lay one piece of polka-dot fabric across one short edge of the cotton panel, raw edges matching and right sides facing. Sew them together with a ⅝" (1.5cm) seam allowance. Open out and press. Attach the other band to the opposite end of the cotton panel in the same way to give a long white panel with a polka dot band at each end.

3 Cut the towelling in half widthwise to give two 20" (50cm) lengths. Sew them back together again with a ⅝" (1.5cm) seam allowance, matching short edges and leaving a 4" (10cm) opening.

4 Match one short end of each length of toweling to the long raw edge of one of the

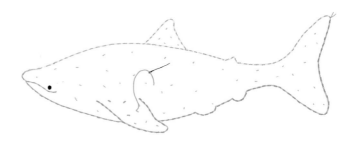

bands of polka-dot fabric. Sew them together with a ⅝" (1.5cm) seam allowance. Open and press.

5 Lay the work out with the toweling right side down, and the sheeting and polka-dot fabric right side up. Fold the strip in half lengthwise, right sides of the sheeting facing. Press.

6 Mark the position of the drawstring casing with two points on each long side of the back. Mark the first one on the sheeting-polka-dot fabric seam and the second one 1¼" (3cm) up from the seam.

7 Pin, baste, and sew together the long sides of the bag with a ⅝" (1.5cm) seam, leaving openings for the drawstring casings. Turn the

bag right side out through the opening in the towelling and slip stitch to close. Push the lining inside the bag and press.

8 Draw two parallel lines with the water-soluble marker to join the openings for the drawstring casing on both sides of the bag. Sew a row of machine or neat handstitching along each line around the bag.

9 Thread one end of the piping through the casing, taking it all around the bag once, and then further to bring it out of the opening on the opposite side. Adjust the cord so that the ends are the same length. Knot both ends of the cord separately and sew each end firmly to one of the bottom corners of the bag.

COLOR GUIDE

gray
317

ivory
387

turquoise
996

primrose
3078

dark smoke
3760

jade
3816

sunflower
3821

medium blue
3843

TEMPLATES

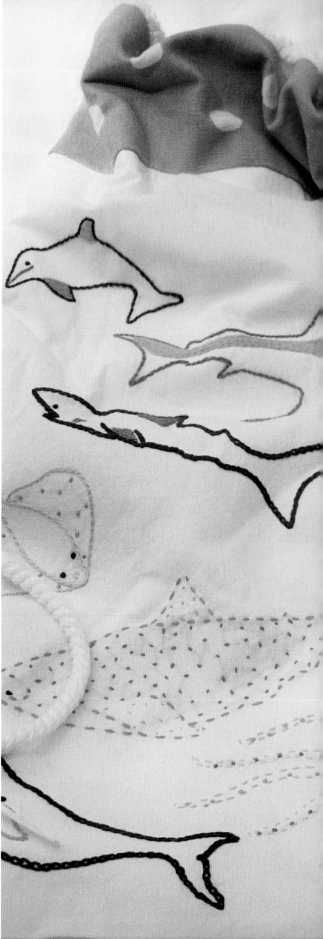

how to make

SAILEY the sailor

A few basic stitches will create this washable sailor doll with a vintage feel. He has bags of character and will make a totally unique and secret friend for a lucky child.

FINISHED SIZE 12"x12" (30cmx30cm), with arms outstretched

MATERIALS AND TOOLS

- DMC stranded embroidery cotton in the following shades:
  half a skein of each color – **349** red; **433** brown; **778** light mauve; **792** damson; **801** chocolate; **3328** strawberry red
- 20"x20" (50cmx50cm) white cotton fabric
- 3¾"x7½" (9cmx18cm) striped ticking or old tea towel for the sailor's vest
- Water-soluble marker
- Dressmakers' carbon paper
- Embroidery hoop
- Crewel needle, size 8
- Dressmakers' pins
- Contrasting thread for basting
- Matching thread for sewing
- Polyester fiberfill stuffing
- Poly pellets

Give Sailey vintage character by using old cotton sheeting and striped ticking.

TECHNIQUES A basic knowledge of either hand or machine sewing is needed. For all embroidery techniques, see pages 114, 116, 118–22.

STITCHES USED Chain stitch, running stitch, satin stitch, split stitch

TEMPLATES

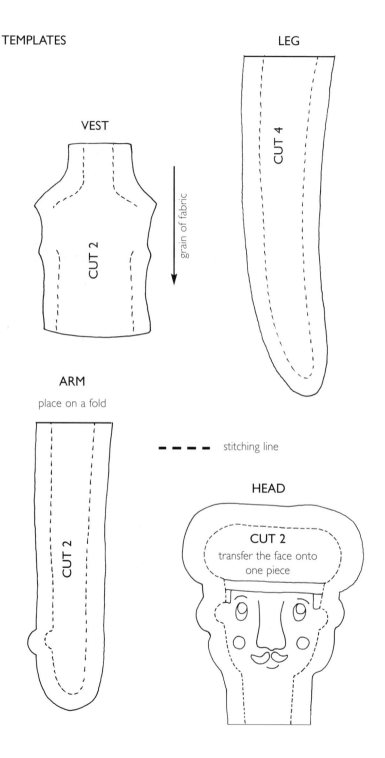

VEST

CUT 2

grain of fabric

LEG

CUT 4

ARM

place on a fold

CUT 2

- - - - stitching line

HEAD

CUT 2

transfer the face onto one piece

To begin the sailor

1 Fold and press the white cotton fabric in half. Cut along the folded line to make two panels.

2 Enlarge the templates to 200%. Place the templates for the arms, on the fold as shown, and the legs onto one panel. Cut around the outer lines and open out the arms. Press flat.

3 Transfer the head outline and details for the face onto the same piece of fabric. Don't cut out the head yet, as you will need extra fabric to stretch into the embroidery hoop.

4 Transfer the vest pattern onto the striped fabric and cut it out.

Working the embroidery

1 Using two strands in the needle throughout, begin by working the lines of the eyebrows, around the eyes, and along the outline of the nose in chocolate split stitch. Fill in the colored area of the eye, the moustache, and the sideburns in brown satin stitch.

2 In light mauve, work a split stitch line for the mouth and satin stitch to fill in the cheeks and nose.

3 Work a band of satin stitch in damson along the rim of the hat. You may wish to work a row of split stitch on either side of the band first to give a neat edge to the satin stitch.

Making the sailor

1 Cut out the head pieces. With right sides facing and edges matching, place the two head pieces together and sew along the seam line, leaving the base of the neck open. Turn the head right side out.

2 Hand sew a row of invisible running stitches in matching cotton thread along the bottom edge of the hat band to prevent the stuffing

The pompom is very simply made with individual looped stitches in red stranded cotton.

COLOR GUIDE

■	red 349
■	brown 433
▨	light mauve 778
■	damson 792
■	chocolate 801
▨	strawberry red 3328

from spreading into the hat. Stuff the head lightly with fiberfill, not forgetting to manipulate it into the ears. Tuck in the opening at the neck and hand stitch to close.

3 Place the two arms right sides together and sew around the seam line, leaving an opening of about 1¼" (3cm) in the middle. Turn the arms right side out. Stuff from the hands to the elbows with poly pellets, carefully pushing the pellets into the thumbs. Then stuff from the elbows to the center with fiberfill. Tuck in the raw edges and hand sew the opening closed.

4 Place the two pieces for each leg right sides together and sew around each seam, leaving the tops of the legs open. Turn the legs right-side out

and stuff them with poly pellets to about 2"
(5cm) from the top of each leg. Finish stuffing
the legs by plugging each one with fiberfill to
within ⅜" (1cm) of the top edge. Neatly tuck
in the raw edges and sew the openings.

5 Place the striped vest pieces right sides
together. Sew along the side and shoulder
seams, leaving an opening at the armholes
and neck as shown. Turn the vest right side
out and tuck in the raw edges. Turn under a
⅜" (1cm) hem around the base edge and
press to hold.

6 Insert about ⅜" (1cm) of the tops of the legs
at the bottom edge of the vest. Check that
the legs are the same length and pin them in
place. Work a running stitch in cotton thread
along the hemmed edge of the vest to join
the back and front of the vest together at the
base, securing the legs at the same time.

7 Work fiberfill into the vest through the
armholes, from the base of the vest up to the
armhole opening. Insert the arms. Continue
to stuff around and above the arms through
the neck opening.

8 Insert about ⅝" (1.5cm) of the neck into the
vest and baste it into position. By now the
head should not flop back and forth but be
able to hold its own weight. If this isn't the
case, stuff a little more fiberfill into either the
neck or the body cavity. Oversew the head
and arms neatly to secure them to the vest
and remove the basting and any pins.

9 To complete the sailor, make a small
pompom for the top of his hat with several
individual looped stitches. Using two strands
of red thread at a time, fold them in half and
then thread the unfolded ends through the
needle. Insert the point of the needle into

the top of the hat and then start to bring the
needle out again slightly to one side of the
first hole. Push the tip of the needle through
the loop of thread and continue to pull the
thread through until the loop lies on top of
the hat. Continue to make seven or eight
looped stitches in the same way. Trim the
ends to about ⅜" (1cm) and fluff up the
pompom (see the photograph on page 85).

Making the clothes

1 Enlarge the templates to 200%. Transfer the
patterns for the clothes onto the remaining
panel of white cotton fabric, so that the
pants, shirt back, and sleeves are on the fold,
as indicated on the templates. Cut out all the
pieces except the shirt front.

2 To embroider the shirt front, use three
strands of strawberry red. Work a line of
chain stitch around the front "v" of the shirt
and the knot at the point in satin stitch. Cut
the shirt front out along the outer lines.

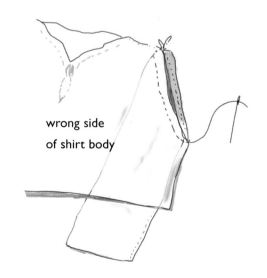

**wrong side
of shirt body**

TEMPLATES

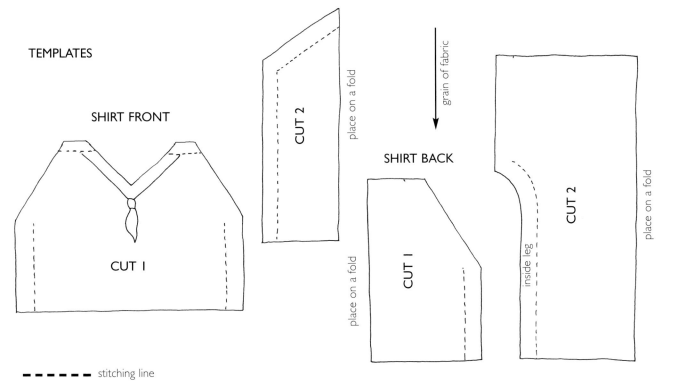

SHIRT FRONT

CUT 1

CUT 2

place on a fold

grain of fabric

SHIRT BACK

place on a fold

CUT 1

inside leg

CUT 2

place on a fold

▬ ▬ ▬ ▬ ▬ stitching line

3 To make the shirt, first open out the shirt back. Place the shirt back and front right sides together with the edges matching. Sew along the side and shoulder seams. Leave these pieces wrong side out.

4 Sew up each sleeve along the side seams, leaving the shoulder seams open. Turn the sleeves to the right side. Insert a sleeve into one of the arm openings on the shirt and pin or baste it in position. Sew around the armhole with a ³⁄₁₆" (0.5cm) seam allowance (see illustration at left). Insert the other sleeve in the same way.

5 Turn under a ³⁄₁₆" (0.5cm) double hem on the bottom edges of the sleeves and, using two strands of strawberry red thread, work a row of running stitch close to the edge of each cuff. Finish the hems at the neck and bottom of the shirt in the same way.

6 Sew up the inside seams for each pant leg and turn one leg right side out. Place one leg

inside the other, right sides facing, and sew around the front and back seams. Turn under a ³⁄₁₆in (0.5cm) hem around the bottom edge of each trouser leg and work running stitch to secure them. Turn under ³⁄₁₆in (0.5cm) around the waist and work gathering stitch all around.

7 Slip the shirt and trousers onto the sailor. Pull the gathering stitch around the waist of the pants to fit, and tie in a knot.

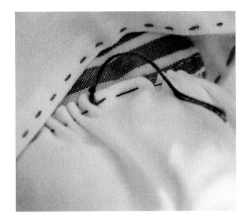

Draw up a gathered thread around the waist of the pants for a perfect fit.

This delightfully tiny fabric doll is just the right size to take everywhere – in a pocket!

how to make
LITTLE pocket mermaid

The vibrant, sweet colors and the small size of this doll make her an absolute gem. Any little girl would adore her and, what's more, she will travel like candy in your pocket. Sweet!

FINISHED SIZE 4⅞" (12cm) high × 6½" (16cm) wide, with arms outstretched

MATERIALS AND TOOLS

- DMC stranded embroidery cotton in the following shades:
  one skein of each color – **165** pear; **225** light shell pink; **369** medium green; **603** bubblegum; **721** orange; **728** orange juice; **796** royal blue; **3816** jade; **3819** apple
- 8"×12" (20cm×30cm) white cotton sheeting
- Remnant of green rickrack for the tail
- Water-soluble marker
- Embroidery hoop
- Crewel embroidery needle, size 6
- Straw (milliners') needle, size 2
- Dressmakers' pins
- Contrasting thread for basting
- Matching thread for sewing
- Polyester fiberfill stuffing

TECHNIQUES A basic knowledge of either hand or machine sewing is needed. For all embroidery techniques, see pages 114, 116–22.

STITCHES USED Bullion knot, French knot, padded satin stitch, satin stitch, split stitch, straight stitch

TEMPLATES

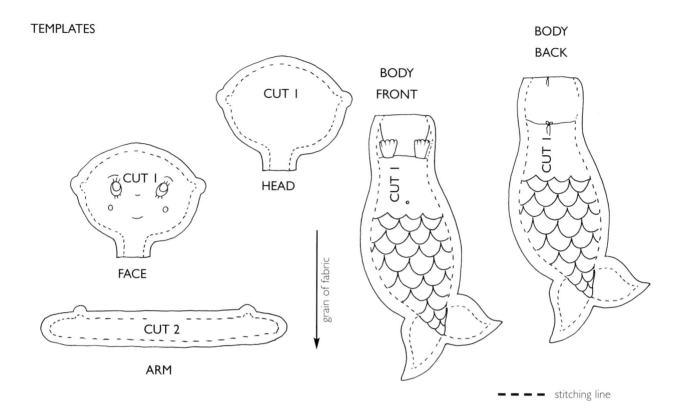

CUT 1

HEAD

BODY FRONT

BODY BACK

CUT 1

CUT 1

CUT 1

grain of fabric

FACE

CUT 2

ARM

- - - - stitching line

Satin stitch creates the perfect effect for the scales. Border each one with split stitch to give a neat edge.

To begin the mermaid

1 Enlarge the templates to 200%. Trace all templates onto the cotton sheeting. Add all the facial features and the tail scales, but don't cut out any of the pieces yet.

Working the embroidery

1 Use two strands for all the embroidery except the tail fins, which are worked in four. Start by working the facial features, referring to the photograph on page 89. Work the lines of the eyebrows in a row of split stitch in orange juice. Work tiny straight stitches in the same color for the eyelashes. Fill in the colored area of each eye in royal-blue satin stitch and work an outline of jade split stitch almost all the way around each eye.

2 For the nose and mouth, continue to work in split stitch, following the curves, in light shell pink and bubblegum respectively. Work the cheeks in light shell pink satin stitch.

3 Stitch five vertical bullion knots in bubblegum to create the two shells for the bikini top (wrap the thread around the straw needle 12 times for each knot). Work three straight stitches underneath each shell. Work one thin line in split stitch in apple between the shells and two more for the neck straps. Embroider a tiny light shell pink French knot for the belly button.

4 Work the tail scales in padded satin stitch in alternate greens and then border them with jade split stitch (see photograph at left).

5 Finally, work the tail fins as "loose" long stitches using four strands of jade thread. Each straight stitch spans the width of the tail fin and is worked close to the next, although not touching, to give the impression that the fins are floating.

Making the mermaid

1 Cut out all the shapes along the cutting lines.

2 Place the two head pieces right sides together and sew around the stitching line, leaving the base of the neck open. Turn the head right side out and stuff it. Tuck in the open end at the neck by about ⅜" (1cm) and hand stitch to close.

3 Place the two arms right sides facing and sew them together, leaving a gap of about 1¼" (3cm) in the middle. Turn the arms right side out and stuff them through the gap. Tuck in the open edges and hand stitch to close.

4 Pin and tack the body pieces right sides together, catching in the rickrack along the edges of the tail. Sew all around the body, leaving the neck and the armholes open. Turn it right side out and baste in the raw edges.

5 Work in the fiberfill up to the armholes. Insert the arms through the opening and then continue to stuff lightly above the arms. Insert the head. Pin, then baste it in position.

Slip stitch the head and the arms to secure them and remove the basting stitches.

6 The hairline runs from the top of one ear to the other ear and along the seam running across the top of the head. Cut eight 5½" (14cm) lengths of each of the orange, orange juice, and bubblegum threads.

7 Using the full six strands, fold one length in half and thread the unfolded raw ends through the needle. Insert the needle into the seam (see illustration 1 below). Push the needle through the fabric and place the looped end over the needle point (see illustration 2 below). Gently pull the thread tight until the loop lies on the seam at the top of the head.

8 Continue attaching the hair along the seam, alternating the colors and working each looped stitch as close to its neighbor as possible. When all 24 strands are securely attached, trim the ends of the mermaid's hair as necessary.

COLOR GUIDE

pear
165

light shell pink
225

bubblegum
603

orange
721

orange juice
728

royal blue
796

medium green
369

jade
3816

apple
3819

1

2

how to make

PIRATE finger puppets and thumb shark

This motley crew will provide a barrel of fun, and couldn't be easier to make.

Frighteningly ferocious, cut-throat, and savage were the pirates of old. However, these fellows are just a bunch of softies. Get ready for some fun and games when you make these jolly character puppets.

FINISHED SIZE Finger width and height

MATERIALS AND TOOLS

- DMC stranded embroidery cotton in the following shades:
  half a skein of each color – **B5200** white; **210** lilac; **310** black; **317** gray; **387** ivory; **433** brown; **778** light mauve; **801** chocolate; **977** rust; **996** turquoise; **3328** strawberry red; **3821** sunflower
- DMC stranded metallic floss: short length of **5284** gold for the earrings
- 2¾"x2¾" (7cmx7cm) white cotton sheeting and/or natural linen scraps for each face
- Various colors of felt and fabric remnants for the arms and hands
- 1⅜"x2" (3.5cmx5cm) black felt for the captain's hat
- 4"x4" (10cmx10cm) gray felt for the shark
- 2" (5cm) length of pipe cleaner for the captain's hook
- Scraps of colored plain or patterned fabrics for the headscarves
- Four different colored elasticized or ribbed cuffs from children's sweatshirts or sweaters
- Dressmakers' carbon paper and/or water-soluble marker
- Embroidery hoop
- Crewel needle, size 6
- Dressmakers' pins
- Contrasting thread for basting stitches
- Matching thread for sewing
- Polyester fiberfill stuffing

TECHNIQUES A basic knowledge of either hand or machine sewing up is needed. For all embroidery techniques, see pages 114, 116, 119–22.

STITCHES USED Blanket stitch, lazy daisy stitch, running stitch, satin stitch, seed stitch, split stitch, straight stitch

TEMPLATES

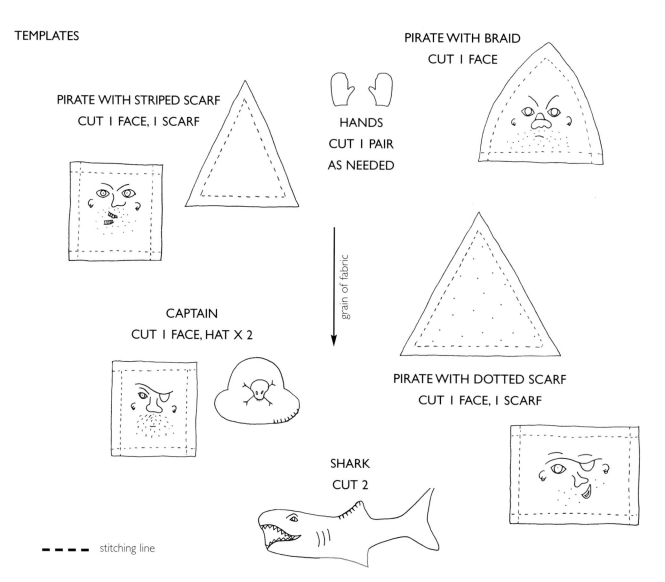

PIRATE WITH STRIPED SCARF
CUT 1 FACE, 1 SCARF

HANDS
CUT 1 PAIR
AS NEEDED

PIRATE WITH BRAID
CUT 1 FACE

grain of fabric

CAPTAIN
CUT 1 FACE, HAT X 2

PIRATE WITH DOTTED SCARF
CUT 1 FACE, 1 SCARF

SHARK
CUT 2

- - - - stitching line

To begin the puppets

1 Enlarge all the templates to 200%. Transfer the faces and outline shapes onto the plain cotton or linen squares.

2 Transfer the triangular headscarves onto appropriate scraps of plain or patterned fabric and keep each scarf with the pirate for which it is intended. Cut out the captain's hat from the black felt.

3 Cut the gray felt in half lengthwise and transfer one shark outline onto each piece.

4 Cut out a pair of hands for each of the three pirates and one hand for the captain from the scraps of colored felt. Form the strip of pipe cleaner into a hook for the captain's other hand.

5 Cut eight ¾"x2¾" (2cmx7cm) strips of colored felt or fabric for the arms. Fold each strip in half widthwise and sew the long side seam, hiding any raw edges and catching in a hand (or the hook for the captain) at one end of each arm.

Embroidering the dotted pirate

1 Using two strands throughout for the pirate with the dotted scarf, work the eyebrows, ears and nose in split stitch in brown. Continuing in the brown, work the seed stitch whiskers.

2 Embroider an earring over the pirate's ear as a single "petal" of lazy daisy stitch in sunflower.

3 Work the straps of the eye patch in split stitch in black and fill in the patch in black satin stitch.

4 Work the mouth in light-mauve split stitch and fill in the mouth with black satin stitch.

5 Work split stitch in sunflower around the open eye. Fill in the eye with turquoise satin stitch and place a single French knot, in black, in the middle for the pupil.

6 Stitch French knots in white on the headscarf to make the dots.

white
B5200

lilac
210

black
301

gray
317

ivory
387

brown
433

light mauve
778

chocolate
801

rust
977

turquoise
996

strawberry red
3328

sunflower
3821

gold
5284

Embroidering the striped pirate

1 Using two strands throughout for the pirate with the striped scarf, work split stitch, in ivory, for the eyebrows. Continuing in split stitch, work gray around the eyes and teeth, rust around the nose and ears, and light mauve along the lips.

2 Fill in the eyes and work the whiskers, in ivory, as for the pirate with the spotted scarf.

3 Work a single lazy daisy stitch earring in gold over both ears and ivory French knots for stubble to complete the face of this pirate.

Embroidering the braided pirate

1 Using two strands throughout for the pirate with the braid (see photograph on page 96), work black split stitch along the eyebrows and around the eyes.

sides facing, and work blanket stitch all around, leaving the bottom edge open.

Embroidering the shark

1 Using two strands throughout for the shark, work along the gums, the scales, and the eyebrows in black split stitch. In white, work the eyes in split stitch and the teeth in straight stitch. Make a black French knot for the center of each eye.

2 Join the two halves of the shark together, wrong sides facing, and work blanket stitch in turquoise all around, but leaving an opening for the thumb. Continue to blanket stitch around both sides of the opening.

2 Outline the nose in split stitch in rust. Fill in the top half of the nose in strawberry red satin stitch and the bottom half in lilac.

3 Work a split stitch mouth in strawberry-red and the whiskers in tiny black seed stitches. Work the earrings as for the other pirates.

Embroidering the captain

1 Using two strands throughout for the captain, work the eye patch in black satin stitch. Stitch his eyebrow and nose in chocolate, his mouth in strawberry red and around his eye in brown – all in split stitch. Work his whiskers in chocolate seed stitch. Fill his eye with turquoise satin stitch. Work the ears and earring as for the pirates, in light mauve and gold respectively.

2 Embroider a skull and crossbones onto one of the hat pieces, referring to the photograph for guidance.

3 Place the two hat pieces together, wrong

To make up your puppets

1 To make up the heads of the pirates with the headscarves, pin and then sew the base edge of the relevant triangle to the top edge of the face, right sides facing, with a ³⁄₁₆" (0.5cm) seam. Press the seam towards the darkest fabric.

2 Fold the face and scarf in half widthwise, right sides facing, and join with a ³⁄₁₆" (0.5cm) seam along the back. Turn right side out.

3 Work a gathering stitch around the neck edge. Stuff the face. Gather up the neck and secure to close. Fold the headscarves to the back of the heads and attach with a couple of stitches.

4 To make the head of the pirate with the braid, fold it in half widthwise and then sew up the back seam. Finish as before.

5 To make the braid, sew six double threads of black through the top of the pirate's head.

Do not secure them but pull them through so the ends are the same length, and then simply braid them to secure them. Tie a bow at the end of the braid to hold it.

6 Put the hat on the captain's head and sew it securely in place.

7 For each of the pirates, cut the cuffs to finger width and height, adding ³⁄₈" (1cm) all around for the seam allowance and ¾" (2cm) allowance for the bottom hem.

8 Turn ³⁄₈" (1cm) at the top edge of the cuff to the right side. Fold the cuff in half, right sides facing, and sew a ³⁄₈" (1cm) seam up the back. Turn a ³⁄₈" (1cm) hem under on the bottom edge and baste, then sew it in place. Turn the cuff right side out. Push the arms into the fold at the top edge and sew them in place. Repeat for the other cuffs.

9 Attach the heads to the bodies by pushing in the gathered edge of the head into the top edge of the finger body and sew securely.

You could adapt this idea to make characters from favorite fairytales or films.

CHAPTER FOUR vintage charm

This is a chic and very feminine collection that makes use of vintage fabrics to create goodies, from dolls and bags to bedding, to give any girlish bedroom just a hint of the stylish past.

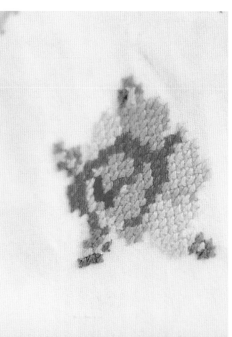

how to make
VINTAGE LADIES

This retro-revival doll for the fashion-conscious child or nostalgic adult is probably one of the easiest dolls to create.

This is possibly the quickest and simplest rag doll you may ever make, and you can alter the colors to match the decor of any room.

FINISHED SIZE 5½" (24cm) high × 2" (5cm) wide, with arms down

MATERIALS AND TOOLS

• DMC stranded embroidery cotton in the following shades:

brown-haired doll one skein of each color, with two of brown – **310** black; **351** dark peach; **433** brown; **605** light cranberry; **796** royal blue; **893** bright pink; **996** turquoise

orange-haired doll one skein of each color, with two of satsuma – **351** dark peach; **433** brown; **605** light cranberry; **796** royal blue; **801** chocolate; **893** bright pink; **996** turquoise; **3340** satsuma

For each of the dolls

• 9½"×11" (24cm×28cm) plain white cotton sheeting

• 5½"×16" (14cm×40cm) patterned fabric

• Water-soluble marker

• Embroidery hoop

• Crewel needle, size 5

• Dressmakers' pins

• Contrasting thread for basting

• Matching thread for sewing

• Polyester fiberfill stuffing

TECHNIQUES A basic knowledge of either hand or machine sewing is needed. For all embroidery techniques, see pages 114, 116–22.

STITCHES USED Lazy daisy stitch, running stitch, satin stitch, split stitch

TEMPLATES

BODY FRONT

BODY BACK

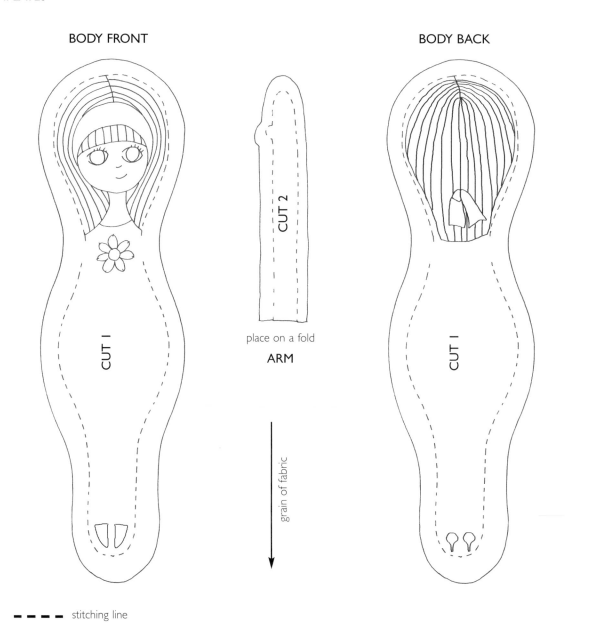

CUT 2

place on a fold

ARM

grain of fabric

CUT 1

CUT 1

- - - - stitching line

COLOR GUIDE

black (brown-haired doll)
310

light cranberry
605

bright pink
893

dark peach
351

royal blue
796

turquoise
996

brown
433

chocolate (orange-haired doll)
801

satsuma (orange-haired doll)
3340

To begin the doll

1 Enlarge the templates to 200%.

2 Transfer the body outlines and the detailed features, using the water-soluble marker to trace them directly onto the white cotton sheeting. Do not cut out the shapes yet.

Embroidering the orange-haired doll

1 Using two strands of chocolate thread, work each eye outline and the nose in split stitch. Then, with two strands of bright pink, work the mouth, again in split stitch. Use three strands of brown thread to fill in the irises of the eyes in satin stitch.

2 With four strands of satsuma, fill in the hair with split stitch on the front and back body pieces. First follow the lines on the template to establish a neat arrangement and then fill in two or three more lines on each side of the first ones so that the overall effect is one of a solid mass of closely knit lines, similar to a block of satin stitch.

3 Work the headband and slippers in four strands of light cranberry in satin stitch.

4 To complete the doll, work the flower motif on the dress in three strands throughout. Embroider the flower center in satin stitch in light cranberry and the petals with seven lazy daisy stitches in bright pink thread. Finish the neckline of the dress in turquoise split stitch.

Embroidering the brown-haired doll

1 To work the brown-haired doll, follow the instructions for the orange-haired doll but make the following color changes. If you wish, you could alter the colors for either doll to match different colored dress fabrics.

2 For the outlines of each eye, work in black; the nose and mouth are in chocolate. Fill in the eyes with royal-blue satin stitch.

3 Work the headband and slippers in turquoise and the hair in brown.

4 Embroider the neckline in dark peach. Give the flower a light-cranberry satin stitch center, but outline the bright-pink petals in split stitch.

A pretty bow attached to the doll's hair adds to her charm, along with her floppy huggable arms.

To make up the doll

1 Cut out the doll shapes along the outer edges of the templates. Cut out two pairs of arms from the white sheeting.

2 With right sides facing, place the two body pieces together. Pin and baste them together. Then sew almost all of the way around the body along the seam line, leaving a 1" (2.5cm) opening on both sides of the body for the arms to be inserted. Turn the body right side out through the arm holes. Stuff the body quite firmly.

3 Place the two arm pieces together and sew all around, leaving a 2" (5cm) opening in the middle for turning through. Trim back the seam allowance to within ⅛" (3mm) of the seam. Turn the arms right side out and press them flat.

4 Thread the arms through the openings in the body. Pull them through until they are the same length. Fold in the raw ends at the armholes and then sew up the openings, securing the arms at the same time.

5 To make the skirt, fold the rectangle of patterned fabric in half widthwise, right sides facing. Stitch up the back with a ⅜" (1cm) seam allowance. Turn the skirt right way out.

6 Turn under a double ⅜" (1cm) hem around the bottom edge of the skirt and machine or hand stitch it in place.

7 Turn in ³⁄₁₆" (0.5cm) to the wrong side around the waist and, starting at the back seam, work a running stitch of embroidery thread all around, about ⅛" (3mm) from the top edge. Do not secure either end, but leave a tail at both ends to allow for gathering and tying the skirt.

8 Slip the skirt over the doll's legs. Draw the running stitch up to gather the skirt around the waist. Tie the thread securely. A few discreet slip stitches will ensure that the skirt stays in place.

how to make
ROSE motif

A simple 1950s-style cross stitch rose will adorn anything you like. Try one on a knitted raffia or wool bag for a dainty flower girl posy.

FINISHED SIZE Depends on stitch size of the knitted item; the design is 21×18 squares

MATERIALS AND TOOLS

- DMC stranded embroidery cotton in the following shades
  one skein of each color – **349** red; **472** pale olive; **603** bubblegum; **772** light lime; **778** light mauve; **906** parrot green; **913** nile green; **3325** light baby blue; **3328** strawberry red; **3609** carnation; **3713** light pink
- Florists' raffia bag, or similar knitted bag
- Crewel embroidery needle, size 5 or 6

TECHNIQUES For all embroidery techniques, see page 118. For how to use the chart, see page 115.

STITCHES USED Counted cross stitch

This vintage motif can be worked on any knitted item, including a raffia bag, or through waste canvas onto any cotton item (see page 115 for details of how to work with waste canvas).

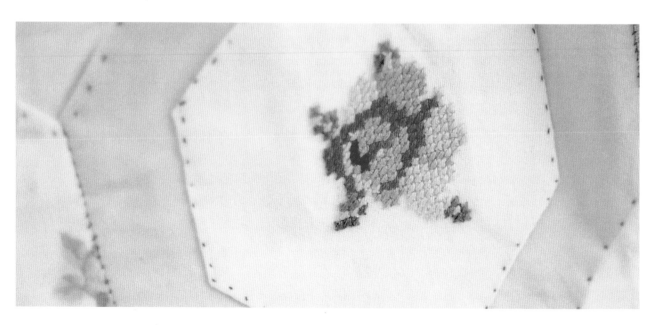

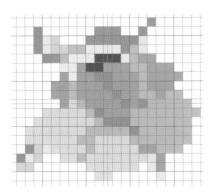

COLOR GUIDE

	light lime 772		carnation 3609
	pale olive 472		bubblegum 603
	nile green 913		light mauve 778
	parrot green 906		red 349
	light baby blue 3325		strawberry red 3328
	light pink 3713		

To work the raffia bag

1 If the bag is similar to the florists' bag pictured here, first remove the plastic liner. Measure and mark the center of the bag.

2 One cross stitch on the chart is worked over one knitted stitch on the bag. Following the chart and using three strands throughout, work cross stitch from the center of the chart (where the red lines cross) and the center point on the bag. Work outward to each corner of the motif. Stitch firmly but not so tightly as to distort the knitted stitches of the bag.

3 When the cross stitch is complete, replace the lining of the bag if desired.

how to make VINTAGE quilt

This quilt is a wonderful way to use up any vintage-style scraps of fabric you may have. It is enhanced with a very individual embroidered motif.

If you're feeling adventurous, embroider two or three vintage ladies in different colors on your quilt.

FINISHED SIZE 40"x56" (100cmx140cm)

MATERIALS AND TOOLS

- DMC stranded embroidery cotton in the following shades:
  one skein of each color – **310** black; **349** red; **747** baby blue; **772** light lime; **778** light mauve; **801** chocolate; **954** pistachio; **996** turquoise; **3821** sunflower
- 9" (23cm) squares × 35 assorted plain, patterned, and floral fabrics, including one of plain white cotton
- 41"x57" (103cmx143cm) plain fabric for the backing
- 40"x56" (100cmx140cm) 4oz batting or twin duvet that can be cut to the finished size
- Water-soluble marker
- Embroidery hoop
- Crewel needle, size 5
- Dressmakers' pins
- Contrasting thread for basting
- Matching thread for sewing

TECHNIQUES A basic knowledge of either hand or machine sewing is needed. For all embroidery techniques, see pages 114, 116–21.

STITCHES USED French knot, lazy daisy stitch, running stitch, satin stitch, split stitch, stem stitch, straight stitch

TEMPLATES

COLOR GUIDE

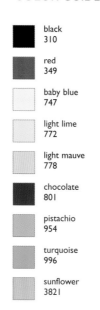

black
310

red
349

baby blue
747

light lime
772

light mauve
778

chocolate
801

pistachio
954

turquoise
996

sunflower
3821

Working the embroidery

1 Enlarge the template to 150%. Transfer the design onto the center of a plain white cotton square of fabric using the water-soluble marker.

2 Use the photograph opposite as a guide for the colors of the embroidery. Start with two strands of chocolate thread and fill in the eyes with satin stitch. Using two strands of black, work split stitch to outline each eye. Then work three tiny straight stitches both above and below the eye outlines to make the eyelashes.

3 Work the nose with two tiny stem stitches, using a single strand of black thread. For the mouth, work a single strand of light mauve in stem stitch. Work around the cheek and chin, the neck, arms, and ankles in stem stitch, using two strands of chocolate.

4 Work a split stitch outline around the dress bodice in three strands of turquoise. With the same color thread, fill in both shoes in satin stitch. Outline the skirt of the dress in three strands of baby-blue split stitch.

5 Embroider the hair in split stitch, using three strands of black. To complete the head, work the hairband in three strands of light lime satin stitch.

6 Work the fan in two strands of sunflower split stitch.

7 All the flowers are worked in three strands. Most are embroidered in satin stitch, but the green, leafy shapes and the daisies on the bottom left of the skirt are worked in lazy daisy stitch. (Refer to the photograph above at right, but use whatever colors you like for individual flowers.)

There's plenty of scope for varying the colors of this enchanting young lady's outfit and giving this quilt a personal touch.

Making the quilt

1 Remove any pen lines on the embroidered square by sponging with a damp cloth and then leaving to dry. Press carefully on the reverse of the embroidery.

2 Arrange all the fabric squares, including the embroidered one, in a pleasing sequence, to give five squares across and seven down. Lightly number the squares on the back to record the sequence.

3 Place the first two squares from the top row right sides facing. Pin and tack them together along one edge, allowing a ½" (1.5cm) seam. Machine or hand stitch the seam. Then open out the squares and press the seam flat. Join the squares for the rest of the top row in the same way.

4 Join the squares to make the other rows of patchwork. Sew the top two strips of squares together, still allowing ½" (1.5cm) seams (see illustration at right). Open out the patchwork and press the new seam flat. Join the other five strips in the same way.

5 Smooth out the backing, wrong side down, on a flat surface. Place the patchwork, right side down, on top. Pin and baste the two panels together.

6 Sew around the edges, allowing a ½" (1.5cm) seam and leaving a 16" (40cm) opening on the bottom edge. Carefully trim the corners to remove excess bulk. Remove the basting stitches. Turn the cover to the right side and gently press on the reverse.

7 If you are using a duvet, cut it to size and oversew the raw edges to keep the stuffing in place. Insert the duvet or batting into the cover and work it into the corners. Hand stitch the opening closed.

8 Hand tie through the quilt at each point where the patchwork squares meet. Using four strands of thread, pass the needle from the top of the quilt to make a stitch and come back up through all the layers twice. Then tie a double knot on the front of the quilt. Neatly trim the ends of the ties to finish.

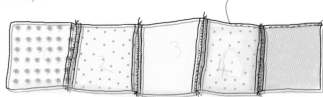

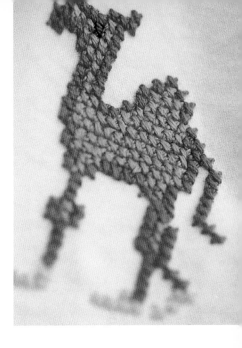

CHAPTER FIVE techniques and stitches

This section contains the information you need to help you make all the projects. Take time out to read through these pages first to make sure you produce superb embroidery of which you can be proud.

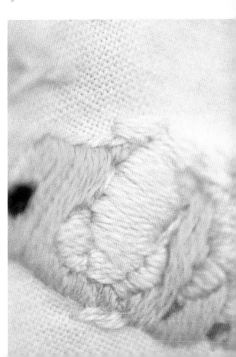

MATERIALS AND EQUIPMENT

The fabric used in this book is, on the whole, plain 100% **cotton sheeting**. Chosen for its close weave and its ability to carry the work well without distortion, cotton sheeting is also widely available and washable – essential for child-friendly items.

Always pre-wash new fabric before cutting it, as shrinkage will generally occur. This said, do try to use old fabrics where possible; for example, an old sheet will provide more than enough fabric to make all the dolls in this book, while an old pair of size 8 jeans will provide the fabric for dear Whaley.

The thread chosen for these projects is **stranded embroidery cotton** (with the exception of pearl cotton for the Farm-edged blanket). Embroidery cotton is available in skeins and consists of six strands loosely twisted together. The strands can be separated, and one or more worked to provide different thicknesses. For example, one strand will give fine facial features, whereas six strands will produce a thick line. Pearl cotton is also twisted but is used straight from the skein and cannot be separated

An embroidery frame of some sort is, in my view, an essential piece of equipment, although you could choose to work without one. However, some stitches, such as satin stitch, will distort if you do not use a frame.

Round wooden hoops are probably

the most appropriate "frames" for the projects in this book. They are widely available and come in a range of sizes, from very tiny to very large. Many types of rectangular frame are also available, so choose one that is right for you.

TIP *Always remember to remove your work from the embroidery hoop between stitching sessions to prevent any permanent marking or creasing.*

Needles must be suitable for the work to get good results. For most of the projects, a **crewel needle** has been used. This is a fine needle with a large, long eye, perfect for piercing the fabric without leaving behind a tell-tale and unsightly hole. Sizes range from 1 to 10 – the lower the number, the larger the eye.

The other types of needle used in the projects are **milliners'** or **straw needles** – perfect for making bullion knots because the eye is no wider than the shaft of the needle – and **tapestry needles**, most suited to embroidering on wool.

TIP *To thread a needle, make sure that the thread has been cut cleanly, fold the end over the eye of the needle, slide off the folded thread, flatten it between your fingers, and push the fold through the eye.*

Other essentials you will need for the projects in this book are: sharp, pointed **embroidery scissors**; **sewing thread** for sewing up, basting, and marker stitches; **dressmakers' pins**; a **tape measure**; and perhaps a **sewing machine** for speed.

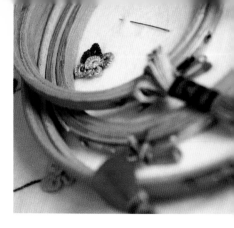

TECHNIQUES

Transfer designs onto fabric after enlarging the design as directed in the project instructions. Press the fabric so that you have an even surface on which to work.

For lightweight fabrics such as cotton sheeting, lay the paper template right side up on a flat surface with the fabric, also right side up, on top. Tape them down if necessary. Use a **water-soluble fabric marker** to trace the design or pattern lines directly onto the fabric. It is important to transfer the whole design before you begin to embroider.

To transfer a design onto heavier fabrics such as denim, use **dressmakers' carbon paper**. Lay the fabric, right side up, on a flat surface and then place the carbon paper, shiny side down, on top. Tape the design in position on top of the carbon paper. Firmly trace over the design with a fine ballpoint pen. Try not to rest your hand heavily on the layers as this may smudge carbon onto the fabric. When the tracing is complete, remove both the carbon and pattern paper.

When the embroidery has been completed, the water-soluble marker or carbon lines can be removed with a damp sponge.

Charted designs are given for the cross stitch projects in this book. They are shown as a grid, marked with colored squares. Each square represents a single cross stitch.

Work the appropriate colors of thread for each cross stitch, referring to the squares on the chart and the accompanying color guide. Work each stitch either over waste canvas, as described below and on the Noah crib sheet, or over knitted stitches, as on the Noah blanket and Rose motif.

TIP *Enlarge the chart on a color copier to make it easier to read.*

Waste canvas makes it possible to work a charted design on any fabric that is not specifically produced for cross stitch, by providing a grid over which stitches can be worked. The starched waste canvas is then carefully stripped out from beneath the worked cross stitches.

Waste canvas is available in different count sizes. The projects in the book all use 14-count canvas, i.e., 14 threads to 1" (2.5cm). It is printed with colored guidelines to help position the design. You will find waste canvas in craft stores, but do not confuse it with tapestry canvas.

To work with waste canvas, first count the number of colored squares, both horizontally and vertically, on the charted design, and then cut a piece of waste canvas at least five squares larger all around. Count the holes or fold the cut piece of canvas in half to find the center

and mark it with a pen or a stitch. Also mark the center point on the fabric so that you can match up the two points.

Lay the canvas on top of the right side of the fabric, matching up the center marks and ensuring that the colored guidelines on the waste canvas are aligned with the grain of the fabric.

Pin and baste the waste canvas in place on the fabric (see illustration 1). An embroidery hoop can be used as long as the waste canvas does not get trapped in the hoops.

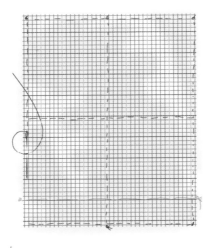

1

Begin stitching the design at the point indicated in the instructions (usually the center) and work each stitch through the center of each hole in the canvas, passing the needle through both the canvas and the fabric (see illustration 2). Where stitches meet, insert the needle through the same hole in the fabric to keep the results neat.

Follow the chart until all the cross stitch has been completed. Then remove the basting stitches and trim the excess

canvas to within ⅜" (1.5cm) of the stitched design. Lightly dampen the canvas

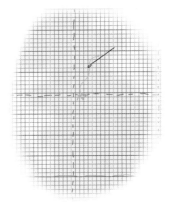

2

and then remove each thread, one at a time. Start with the vertical threads and carefully pull them through with the aid of a pair of tweezers (see illustration 3).

Once all the vertical threads have been removed, the horizontal threads can be gently eased out.

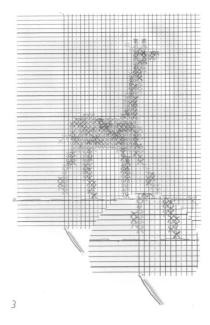

3

How to begin and end your work

Your embroidery should be very neat – on the back as well as the front – and this is easy to achieve using a few simple techniques.

To prevent any tangling and twisting of thread, cut it no longer than 20" (50cm).

Start by securing the thread. First, make a knot in one end and insert the needle from the front to the back about 2" (5cm) away from where you wish to begin, thus leaving a knot on the top surface. As you begin to embroider, stitch over the starting thread on the back of the work. When the thread is secure, cut off the knot and trim the excess.

To finish, weave the threaded needle back through the last few stitches on the reverse side of the work in a neat and secure manner. Cut off any excess.

Looking after your work To keep your work clean while you are working on it, keep the embroidery in a clean bag or pillowcase between stitching sessions.

All the projects in this book can be washed on a gentle spin wash, because all DMC threads are colorfast. However, if an alternative brand of thread is used, check the labeling for washing instructions first. Do not tumble dry your embroidery.

Pressing should be done while the embroidery is still slightly damp. Place the embroidered item face down on a towel and iron the reverse side to avoid flattening the stitches.

STITCHES

The embroidery stitches illustrated and described here are some of the most elementary stitches used, and they are all you need to complete the designs in this book. If you wish, you could substitute different stitches for the ones specified in the projects to create your own personal, embroidered masterpiece. Do not be afraid to try things on a spare piece of fabric. A little experimentation will quickly give you an idea of how the design will look. Then if you like it, go for it!

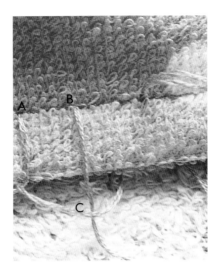

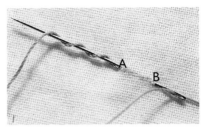

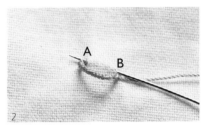

Blanket stitch This stitch is traditionally used as a decorative edging for blankets. It is also used to conceal raw edges on appliqué or buttonholes, in which case the stitches are worked close together and are known as **buttonhole stitch**.

How to work the stitch Secure the thread at the back and bring the needle to the front at A, ready to work from left to right. Take the needle to the back again and come up at B, holding the thread down with your thumb to retain a loop as you do so. Take the needle down under the loop at C. Pull the needle through until the thread touches the edge of the fabric but does not pull it or distort it. Continue in this way along the fabric edge. Secure the thread at the back when the line of stitches is complete.

Bullion knot This stitch consists of a long twisted knot of thread lying on the surface of the fabric.

How to work the stitch Secure the thread at the back and bring the needle through to the front at point A, where you want the top of the knot to be. Determine the finished length of the knot and insert the needle that distance away from A, at B. Come up again at A, taking care not to split the thread. Wind the thread clockwise five times (or other specified number) around the tip of the needle, at the same time pulling the wound thread down toward the surface of the fabric with your index finger (see 1). Pull the thread tight and ease the needle through the coils (see 2), holding on to them as the needle and thread pass through them. Pull the thread away from you to ensure a tight, even knot, and then pull the thread toward B. Tease the coils to make them even, then anchor the knot by taking the needle to the back at B.

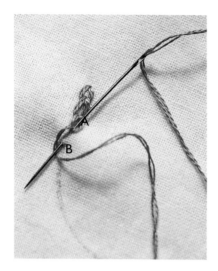

Chain stitch This is a versatile rope-like looped stitch that can be worked either as an outline or as a filling stitch.

How to work the stitch Secure the thread at the back and then bring the needle through to the surface at A, the point where you want the first stitch to be. Hold the emerging thread down with your thumb.

Re-insert the needle at A, still holding down the thread, which has now formed a loop. Bring the needle out at B, thus determining the length of the stitch, and pull it through the loop until the loop lies flat and tightens around the thread. Take care not to pull too tightly. Hold down the emerging thread again and re-insert the needle at B. Continue in this fashion until the chain covers the working line, or work rows of chains, as on the Bobbing boats sheet, to fill in a shape. After the needle has passed through the last loop, anchor the loop with a small stitch and secure the thread at the back.

Cross stitch This stitch is usually worked from a chart either through waste canvas or onto Aida fabric (the classic choice for cross stitch, it is woven so that groups of four interwoven threads form blocks which directly relate to each square on a cross stitch chart).

How to work the stitch To work a single cross stitch, secure the needle at the back and bring it up to the front at A. Take the needle back down at B, making a diagonal stitch. Re-emerge at C and then go back down at D to make the cross stitch.

To work a row of cross stitches, work the half cross stitch from A to B. Then continue making just these diagonal stitches until you have completed the line of that color. Then work back along the same line to complete the second part (from C to D) of each stitch.

All the top threads should run in the same direction.

Fern stitch Useful for making a continuous line or scattered isolated stitches for a filling, fern stitch looks like a little "Y."

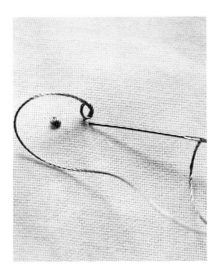

French knot Like a small bead lying on the surface of the fabric, this textural stitch is particularly useful for the dotting of eyes and the centers of flowers.

How to work the stitch Secure the thread at the back and bring the needle through to the front at the point where you want the knot to be. Hold the thread with your other hand and bring it over the needle. Keeping the thread tight, wind it around the needle once if using three or more strands, or twice if using one or two strands.

Still holding the thread firmly, twist the needle point round and insert it back into the fabric very close to where it first emerged. Pull the needle and thread through to the back until the knot lies flat on the fabric and is secure.

TIP *It is worth practicing this knot a few times to make it perfect.*

Lazy daisy stitch A few simple secured loop stitches create an instant flower.

How to work the stitch Secure the thread at the back and bring the needle through at A, the point where the center of the flower is to be. Re-insert the needle at B, very close to the starting point. Draw the thread through to create a loop on the surface of the fabric and hold the loop down with your finger.

Make a straight stitch the length of the required "petal" on the back of the fabric (to C), bringing the tip of the needle through to the front of the fabric and through the loop of thread. Pull the thread until the loop lies flat and forms an attractive petal shape. Anchor the stitch with a small straight stitch.

Continue to work other petals around the center point in the same manner and then secure the thread at the back.

Padded satin stitch A raised and padded effect is created in this variation of satin stitch.

How to work the stitch Before working satin stitch in the usual way, work a series of short straight stitches just inside the outline and randomly across the center of the shape to be filled, creating a foundation that will pad the satin stitch.

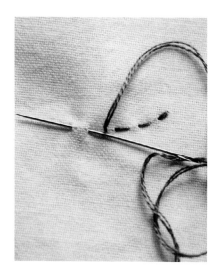
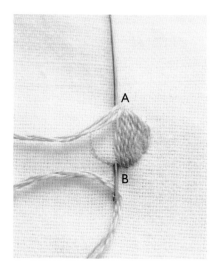
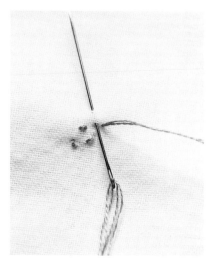

Running stitch Here short stitches run in and out on the surface of the fabric in a single broken line.

How to work the stitch Secure the thread and, working from right to left, pass the needle in and out of the fabric to make a line of short stitches. Keep the stitches and the spaces between even.

Satin stitch This is used for filling small areas with solid color. The stitches are worked closely and neatly together across the shape on the design.

How to work the stitch Bring the needle up on the top edge of the shape to be filled, at A. Insert the needle at the bottom edge, at B. Gently pull the thread through so that it lies flat on the fabric. Bring the needle up at the bottom edge again, close to the start of the first stitch, and repeat the process until the shape has been filled. Keep the stitches neat and parallel, and do not let them overlap, so as to give a smooth block of solid color.

Seed stitch This filling is achieved with tiny random straight stitches.

How to work the stitch Work tiny straight stitches of approximately ⅟₁₆" (1mm) long, scattering them in a random fashion in any direction.

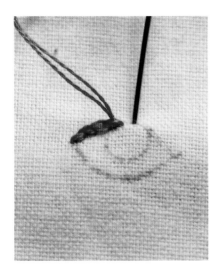

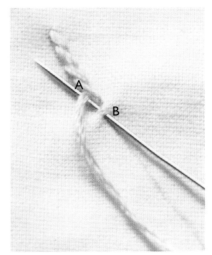

Split stitch This is a versatile stitch for outlining the fine featured elements of a design such as faces, where delicacy is of the essence.

How to work the stitch Secure the thread at the back and bring the needle up at the end of the design line, ready to work from left to right.

Make one short stitch along the design line. Then re-emerge to the front through the center of first stitch, splitting the strands of thread with the needle. Pull the thread through and continue along the line in the same manner.

Stem stitch One of the most frequently used stitches, this is invaluable not only for making flower stems, but also for outlining curves.

How to work the stitch Secure the thread and bring the needle to the front at A, just to the left of the design line. Take the needle back down at B, just to the other side of the line. Pull the thread through so that it creates a slightly diagonal stitch along the design line.

Continue in this way to make a line of stitches that are all the same length.

Straight stitch These single flat stitches form the basis of many other stitches, but can also be worked in their own right to give fine detail to a design.

How to work the stitch Secure the thread at the back and bring the needle through to the front of the fabric. Then take the needle through to the back, making one straight stitch, which can be of any length and in any direction.

CHARTS

The alphabet chart on the right is for the Noah blanket. Either use random letters or work the recipient's name. Plan the name on graph paper first and then work directly onto the blanket, following the instructions in the project.

Use the abc chart below with waste canvas for the Dolly's quilt, following instructions within the project

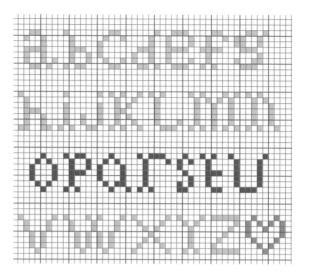

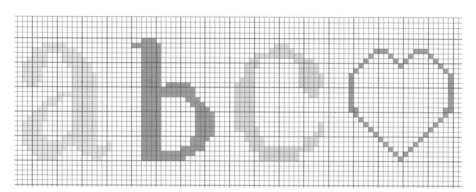

CONVERSION CHART

The designs in this book were embroidered with DMC stranded embroidery cotton. If you prefer to work in Anchor embroidery cotton, refer to the conversion chart below. Please note that it is not always possible to provide exact equivalents.

DMC Anchor

162 - 159	317 - 400	422 - 372	680 - 901	745 - 300	796 - 133	954 - 203	3325 - 129	3760 - 162	3843 - 1089
167 - 375	340 - 118	433 - 358	702 - 226	746 - 275	801 - 359	963 - 23	3328 - 1024	3816 - 876	B5200 - 1
210 - 108	341 - 117	435 - 365	721 - 324	747 - 158	809 - 130	964 - 185	3340 - 329	3817 - 875	white - 2
225 - 1026	349 - 13	472 - 253	726 - 295	761 - 1021	828 - 9159	976 - 1001	3348 - 264	3819 - 278	
301 - 1049	351 - 10	564 - 206	727 - 293	772 - 259	893 - 27	977 - 1002	3609 - 85	3821 - 305	
309 - 42	369 - 1043	603 - 62	728 - 305	778 - 968	906 - 256	996 - 433	3713 - 120	3823 - 386	
310 - 403	413 - 236	605 - 1094	742 - 303	792 - 941	913 - 204	3078 - 292	3755 - 140	3834 - 100	

DMC Pearl Cotton no. 5 shade 729 - Anchor Pearl Cotton shade 888

DMC Stranded Metallic Floss shade 5284 - Anchor Lamé shade 303

DIRECTORY

NOAH CRIB SHEET
Pages 10–15

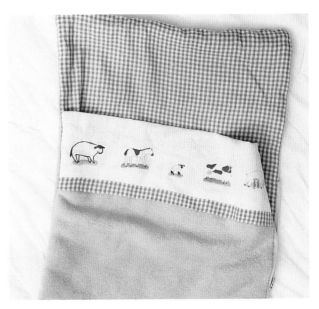

BABY SNUGGLE BAG
Pages 16–21

NOAH BLANKET
Pages 10–15

FARM-EDGED BLANKET
Pages 22–5

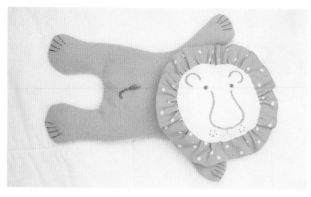

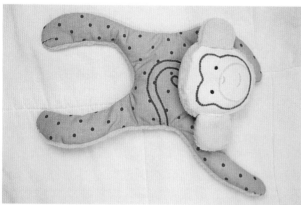

ANIMAL CUDDLERS
Pages 26–33

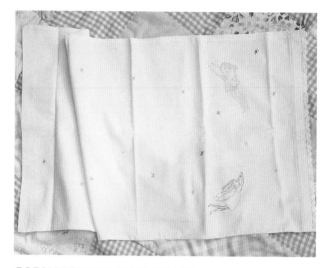

DREAMY FAIRIES PILLOWCASE
Pages 40–5

SO-SOFT SLIPPERS
Pages 34–7

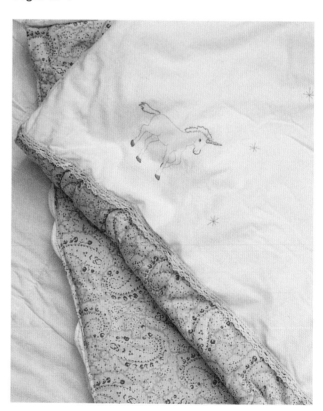

UNICORN QUILT
Pages 40–5

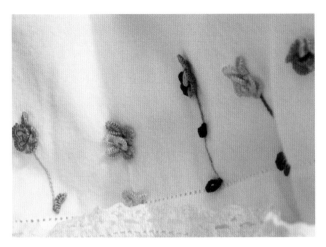

FLOWER GARDEN BORDER

Pages 46–51

DOLLY'S QUILT

Pages 58–61

LITTLE PRINCESS DOLL

Pages 52–7

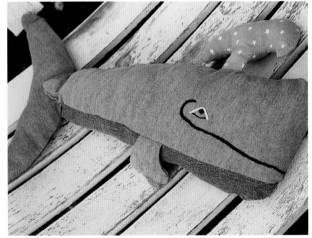

WHALEY THE WHALE

Pages 64–7

BOBBING BOATS SHEET

Pages 68–71

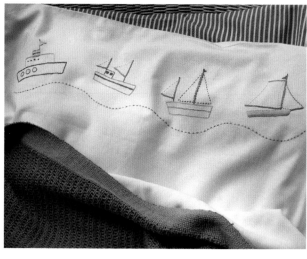

BOATY PILLOWCASE

Pages 72–5

WHALES AND DOLPHINS BEACH BAG

Pages 76–81

SAILEY THE SAILOR

Pages 82–7

LITTLE POCKET MERMAID

Pages 88–91

VINTAGE LADIES

Pages 100–5

ROSE MOTIF

Pages 106–7

PIRATE FINGER PUPPETS AND THUMB SHARK

Pages 92–7

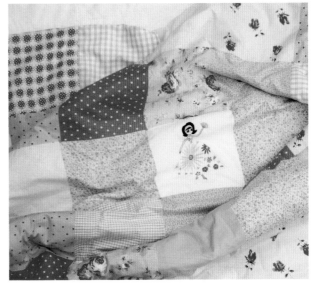

VINTAGE QUILT

Pages 108–11

INDEX

Page numbers in **bold** refer to projects

ACKNOWLEDGMENTS

My sincerest thanks to Anna at Mitchell Beazley for having the vision, enabling me to realize my passion for all things creative; without your generous support these ideas, this book, would never have surfaced and remained a dream. I am greatly indebted, also, to Auberon and Tim for your excellent guidance and for putting it all together, and to Karen for your meticulous checking, clever words, and gentle teaching to this novice. To all – a joy to work with such professionals. I would also like to thank Cath Kidston Ltd for their kind permission to use their fabrics for some of the projects.